storm shelter tower on Triglav summit

Spomenik Padlim Partizanom Gornikom

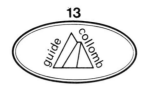

Julian Alps

MOUNTAIN WALKING

AND OUTLINE CLIMBING GUIDE

ROBIN G. COLLOMB

West Col

JULIAN ALPS

First published in this edition 1990 by
West Col Productions
Goring   Reading   Berks.   RG8 9AA

Copyright © 1978,1982,1990 West Col Productions

Drawings and diagrams by
Stephanie Collomb, Patricia Ellis

SBN   906227 41 0

Printed in England by Swindon Press Ltd
Swindon   Wilts.

Contents

Illustrations

ABBREVIATIONS

biv.	bivouac (hut)
c.	approximately
CAI	Italian Alpine Club
FB	Freytag-Berndt (map)
Ger.	German
Gr.	Grade (of difficulty)
h.	hour(s)
IGM	Italian military map
Ital.	Italian
KK	Kompasskarte (map)
km.	kilometre(s)
L	left (direction)
m.	metre(s)
min.	minute(s)
M.	Monte
mtn.	mountain
ÖK	Austrian ordnance map
pt.	point (spot height)
PZS	Slovene Mountain Association
R	right (direction)
rte(s).	route(s)
Slov.	Slovene
TCI	Italian Touring Club

Compass directions are indicated as N, S, E, W, NE, SW, etc.

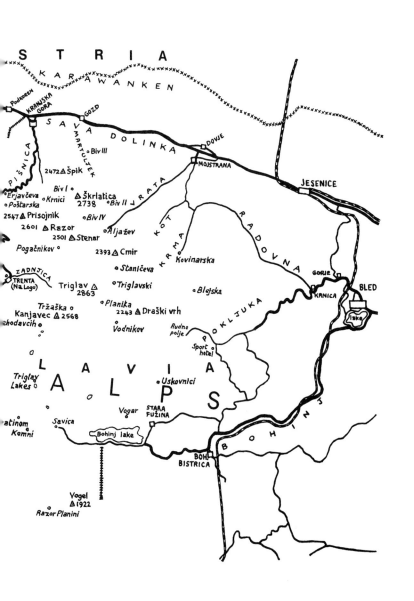

Introduction

GENERAL

The Julian Alps (in which the colony of Forum Julii was settled after one of Julius Caesar's marches to subdue troublesome borders of the Roman empire) have been rarely visited by British alpinists either before or after the Second World War. Rock climbing interest in the Eastern Alps has been almost entirely captured by the larger adjoining area of the Dolomites, and to a lesser extent the Northern Limestone Ranges of Austria. Annual visits by mountain walking parties can be roughly estimated as five groups each year for the last 20 years. Since 1975 the Ramblers' Association has sent three parties each year to follow a prearranged high level route with diversions to attractive summits. Rock climbers have occasionally visited the N face of Triglav (first climbed by a British party in 1936) in the course of travelling in the Eastern Dolomites, but otherwise few reports have been published of British climbing elsewhere in the region. A local guide declared in 1977 that the British were seen on Triglav every year for 10 years in the period c. 1955-1965 and have since 'disappeared'.

This picturesque rocky group is one of the finest limestone regions in the Alps; it forms the most easterly and southerly of the constituent Alpine ranges as defined by Coolidge. The continuous W-E sub-chains of the Carnic and Karawanken Alps bound the N side of the region and so mark the Austrian frontier as it is drawn today. A popular misconception places the Julian Alps in Yugoslavia whereas about half the defined mtn. zone - the W half - lies in Italy. Thus the region is divided NE-SW from the Austrian border by a diagonal ridge marking the Italian-Yugoslav boundary. This ridge is crossed by an historical pass, the Predil, now a good road, which remains the most direct communication for travellers between the two parts of the range.

It is due to no accident that the Italian part is virtually unknown to British mountaingoers. The very active Yugoslav tourist body called 'Kompas' has ensured for the last quarter of a century that in promoting the Julian Alps to holidaymakers only Triglav and its immediate surroundings in the eastern part are worthy of our attention. Needless to say the Italian part, though less romantic in its mountaineering lore, is comprised of equally impressive limestone scenery besides having the second highest summit in the range, the Jôf di Montasio. Its N wall aspect is every bit as magnificent as any other rockface in the Julians.

War and political horse-trading finally won much of the present Yugoslav Julians from the Austro-Hungarian empire and Italy in turn. Now properly Slovenia - the most NW province of Yugoslavia - the loftiest section of the range is compressed in the most north-westerly corner of the province and remains hemmed in on two sides by Italy and Austria to the W and N respectively.

Julius Kugy (1858-1944), a native of Trieste (but Austrian by birth) and the first great explorer of the Julian Alps, is a name both synonymous with the region and eponymous in much of the mtn. topography encountered by the scrambler and climber. His expeditions between 1885-1910 are recorded in the much admired autobiographical book Alpine Pilgrimage, translated into English and published by Murray in 1934, and regarded by many as a classic in mtn. literature equal to Whymper's Scrambles. In a large measure Kugy had been inspired to devote his exploratory instincts to the region on discovering commentary about the Julian Alps in the Gilbert & Churchill book, The Dolomite Mountains, issued as far back as 1864. Suggestions in recent English literature that his name is forgotten in Slovenia are nonsense. His contribution is alive in all informed minds and a unique monument to him has been erected in the upper Trenta valley.

LANGUAGE

Four languages are commonly spoken in the Eastern Julians while only Italian and a little German are heard in the Western part. The Italian zone is a poor region economically and the tourist industry has failed to embrace it fully. The Slovenes have their own Slav language while the official language of Yugoslavia is Serbo-Croat. Both are Cyrillic tongues with the use of an accent over letters to emphasise sounds that are not possible using the Roman alphabet to which both are converted in modern usage. Slovene is particularly difficult in pronunciation for persons only accustomed to Western European languages like English, French, German, Italian. Letters representing vowels or vowel applications are quite different and more numerous in the Slav languages - an inheritance from the former Greek alphabet. Also in the Julian Alps the Slovenes nearly always speak German and Italian, acknowledging that former territorial annexations are within living memory. Their economy and lifestyle is much dependent upon and influenced by the proximity to Western European society - clearly to a more marked extent than the rest of the socialist republic of Yugoslavia. As a 'democratic' communist state Yugoslavia has remained outside the East European 'block' since the end of World War II.

British relationships with the Yugoslav people and especially the Slovenes are good. British visitors are warmly welcomed and are treated in the manner one is accustomed to say in Switzerland. Contrary again to recent reports in magazine articles English is fairly widely spoken or understood where it matters - in hotels, tourist offices, mtn. inns and among some hut wardens, though seldom by shop assistants where basic German or Italian must suffice. French is almost un-known.

German and Italian names have been expunged from the Yugoslav Julians but persist in some local usage and printed references. The most notable retention of an Italian name appears in the Trenta valley where the village centre of Na Logu has been renamed officially Trenta in 1973. However many older names linger on and in the local dialect Triglav comes out sounding like 'Trickala'. A glossary of Slovene names and terms has been included in the guide, and in mtn. and route descriptions former names are given for summits, passes, etc.

PLACE NAMES

Peculiarities of Slovene determine sometimes that certain topographical features are not qualified; good examples are:

Vršič - the name of an important road pass, but not called 'pass' as such.

Vrata - the name of an important valley, but not qualified in the language as a 'valley'. (Both these names crop up in the naming of other topographical features which often bear no similarity to the features cited above). It follows that what we know as the definite article is not used before such names, as in the example, 'we crossed the Vršič pass'. In Slovene they would say, 'we crossed Vršič' and 'we went up (to) Vrata'. The rule is frequently but not always broken in the guide by adding the definite article and qualifying the name. Explan-ations of place names are also given in the glossary and under main headings in the guide.

CHARACTER OF REGION

The limestone of the East Julians is mainly of the karstic variety, massive and sculptured into fantastic shapes including crazy pinnacles, immense holes and caves; the West is more dolomitic in character but equally rugged. The rock is noted for its brilliant whiteness and seen from a distance the blending of features presents an aggravating problem for photographers. The rock is slightly better in quality than the norm accepted for the Dolomites but inevitably low-angled faces, easy ridges and rock walls cut by flights of terraces are shattered, loose and sometimes dangerously crumbling. The excellence and quality of some of the rock climbing areas equal Chamonix granite. The chief summits are composed of solid rock and are approached by engineered paths equipped artificially; stripped of these fixtures pitches of grade II and III might have to be climbed. Cliffs descend a long way into valleys and cause paths to make tortuous circuits along exposed slopes. Such places are always protected by metal ropes and large iron spikes. Valley slopes are forested to a considerable height and a jungle belt of dwarf-pine clothes higher slopes before open areas of grass and scree are encountered. Dwarf-pines entwine everything round them like an octopus' tentacles. The intervention of large rock barriers everywhere forces traverse paths in particular to make numerous descents before gaining real height and the ultimate objective. Reascents on return routes are notorious among walking parties in the Julians.

Many small lakes are found in high cwms and rarely at lower heights, although the only large lake, Bohinj, is at only 500m. where the forest belt is beautifully open and full of spacious park-like glades. Water is scarce in many of the upper valleys because in summer stream beds are dry. Water runs underground and re-emerges in the middle and lower valleys. Springs are tapped in high locations and water can be had from snowmelt. Fairly large snowfields are found right through summer but vary much according to season and weather. Considerable snow may be retained until end July, and the region equates more in this respect to one of 3200m. in the Central Alps, instead of 2800m. in the Eastern. Triglav's 'Green Snow' glacier is much reduced and is no larger than other permanent snowfields. Monte Canin has a considerable glacier-type snowfield. Moderately steep snow slopes may be crossed or ascended on normal routes and an ice axe is essential for protection in the sense of a secure walking stick. It can be dispensed with on routes devoid of snowfields. A few climbs in the true meaning of the term utilize steep snow couloirs - Jalovec N route is a good example.

While the Julian Alps barely exceed 2800m. the vertical interval between valleys and huts, thence to summits, is much the same as ascents in the Western Alps. Valley bases have an altitude of 500 to 800m., therefore a rise of 1000m., sometimes much more, to a high hut is common enough, and $3\frac{1}{2}$-$4\frac{1}{2}$ h. is a normal time for hut walks. Hut to summit times are generally a good deal less when following normal routes and 2-3 h. is usual.

The ascent of graded rock climbs is a lesser activity in the Julians than mtn. walking. The discrepancy is wider than say in the Dolomites. In Slovenia mtn. walking is called 'mountaineering', and the high level traverse variety across passes from hut to hut is widely practised. Indeed the siting of huts encourages this activity while special smaller bivouac shelters have been erected in rock climbing areas which are off the 'trade' routes. Distances between huts for high level touring rarely exceed 5-6 h. and may be much less. Traverses can be made along slopes, ridges and over passes, while diversions to summits are often taken without much additional effort. The general standard is comparable with scrambling on the main ridge of the Black Cuillin (Skye) but the feeling of exposure may be greater; the size of the landscape is approximately double. For a further comparison the Crib Goch and Crib y Ddysgl ridge of Snowdon are of a distinctly inferior standard.

Contrary to popular opinion summer weather in the Julians can be as fickle and variable as most other places in the Alps. July to mid September is the best period but August is prone to rainy spells and thunderstorms. Early September is traditionally a time of settled weather; then also snowfields have diminished and need hamper no one.

The flora of the Slovene Julians is renowned and large warning notices in four languages (but not English) are posted near the start of many popular trails to deter flower pickers. This ruling is rigorously enforced in the areas designated nature reserves (in Slovene terminology called 'parks'). The mtns. are also full of chamois, mostly tame enough to approach a quiet party - the present author had his hat eaten by one that calmly descended a grade III ridge to sniff a piece of cheese laid out as bait; unfortunately it chose among other items scattered on a ledge the hat.

TOPOGRAPHY

See sketch map, pp. 8-9. The principal tourist resorts and centres of the East Julians are Kranjska gora (N), Bled and Stara Fužina (E and S) and Trenta (W); the latter is not really a village resort, more a departure point; Bovec is the village centre below the Trenta valley area but this is rather distant to use as a base. In the West Julians the head of the Nevea saddle pass on the S side of the range is the best starting point; villages in the lower valleys are rather scattered in relation to the main summits and none of them except Valbruna (N side) serve more than one major peak. With a restricted bus service in the West Julians the motorist has a distinct advantage.

The chief summits in the East Julians are: Triglav (2863m.), Škrlatica (2738m.), Jalovec (2643m.), Razor (2601m.), Kanjavec (2568m.) and Prisojnik (2547m.); the latter is probably the most ascended mtn. in the region. Other fine tops include

Špik (2472m.), Stenar (2501m.), Križ (2410m.), Mojstrovka (2369m.) and Travnik (2379m.), though some of these will only draw rock climbers.

Along the diagonal dividing ridge of the Italian and Yugoslav Julians, and almost at opposite ends, are the important summits of Mangrt (2677m.) and Monte Canin (2587m.). The West Julians are dominated by the magnificent Jôf di Montasio (2754m.), Jôf Fuart (2666m.) and M. Cimone (2379m.). Many tower-like summits in this area of 2000-2500m. are the preserve of rock climbers.

The Trenta valley (Soča or Isonzo river, spelt variously) is one of the two or three main inroads to the Julian Alps, and runs up under the E side of the diagonal dividing ridge to cross the W-E watershed at the Vršič pass, thence N down the Pišenca (Pišnica) valley to Kranjska gora. Access to this area round the N side of the range in Yugoslavia is direct and quick from Ljubljana, through Kranj, Jesenice and Dovje (Mojstrana) to Kranjska gora, by bus along a fast but very busy motor road. Before Jesenice, along a road spur W, is the famous resort of Bled, leading in turn by road and rail to the Lake Bohinj area and Stara Fužina on the S side of Triglav. The present roadhead is at the Dom Savica (inn). Also mounting from Bled is an eastern road approach to Triglav, through the zone called Pokljuka - one of the more depressing forest areas of the Julians, now being cleared for a winter sports development - to a roadhead at Rudno Polje. This is merely an approach and not a centre for excursions, although a good traverse combination may be commenced from here.

The Koritnica valley N of Bovec leads up by road over the Predil pass to the Italian Val Rio del Lago. Lower down this valley is the rather poor but large village of Cave del Predil while higher up the Nevea pass (hotels, inn, mtn. hut) offers the easiest approach to main summits in the West Julians. This valley can be entered from the bottom at Tarvisio by following the main Ljubljana-Kranjska gora road W into Italy. Similarly by continuing beyond Tarvisio one soon reaches the entrance to the charming Valbruna and a roadhead at Malga Saisera (inn).

ACCESS

From Britain the quickest way to the Julian Alps is to fly direct to Ljubljana (2 h., the airport is near Brnik, about 20 km. N of the city, and much nearer to Kranj - 7 km.), thence by bus or train to ultimate destination. Avis and Hertz operate car hire from the airport (expensive, plus 16% tourist tax in 1977) which can be paid for in advance in Britain. Few will undertake the long overland rail journey from a channel port which entails changing at least twice by the best services across Germany and Austria with a final section by bus.

An alternative approach and the cheapest by far for a party of three or more is to buy a fly/drive ticket from London to Venice Marco Polo airport ($1\frac{3}{4}$ h.), and with the car as part of the inclusive package fare, drive to the Julians - half a day's easy motoring. Peak season cost for a party of three in 1977 for two weeks = £130 return per head with no extras apart from petrol running costs. All vehicle documentation is prepared in advance and simply collected at the airport on arrival.

MOUNTAIN ROADS AND MOTORING

Roadways in the main valleys are generally narrow and pot-holed in Yugoslavia, somewhat better in Italy. Visitors with cars larger than 1800cc may find driving hazardous. Fairly numerous side roads into the upper mtn. valleys are very narrow, rutted and have no surface; they are littered with stones and small rocks and have few passing places. One in four gradients and sharp, steep slithery bends are common. Some of these roads in Yugoslavia carry bus services and it is a wise precaution to check timetables at the bottom or top before proceeding in a car. Petrol stations are few in Yugoslavia, more frequent in Italy, and the tank should be filled at every opportunity. Even a small car only averages 15-20 miles per gallon in mostly 2nd gear work on these roads. Petrol is 30% cheaper in Yugoslavia compared with Italy (1977). A British driving licence is acceptable in both countries coupled with Green Card insurance.

VALLEY TRANSPORTATION

In Italy buses are infrequent and alternative local taxi services expensive. In Yugoslavia buses are almost hourly everywhere and relatively cheap, operating in the main valleys about 8 times a day and even 4 times across the Vršič pass. Good connections exist between trains and buses in the lower valleys. Supplementary taxi services are easy to come by.

MOUNTAIN INNS AND HUTS, MOUNTAIN RESORT HOTELS

With a few exceptions noted in the guide self-catering/cooking is not permitted in Italian or Slovene huts. Cold foodstuffs and beverages taken by visitors to huts may be freely consumed. Most huts in Yugoslavia, but not all, provide hot water for making tea/coffee/instant soup, at a rate in 1977 of about 25p. per litre. Otherwise hot and cold beverages, soft and alcoholic drinks and a fairly varied menu of cooked meals are provided by all the main hut establishments. There is no obligation to buy meals or drinks. Passports and club cards have to be surrendered on booking into Slovene huts but not in Italian ones. Larger huts have drinking water on tap (suspect ?), wash basins, proper toilets and sometimes shower rooms. A shop, television room, separate bar/lounge are provided in some of them. Bivouac huts have locked doors and keys must be obtained as indicated in descriptions. Blankets and bunks for sleeping. Accommodation and facilities in huts are described in the Huts section of the guide. Most huts with a a restaurant service are open from 1 July to 30 September.

A few inns situated in high valleys are conducted like mtn. huts and are comparatively cheap for rest days. Cars can be driven to the door so they are often full but advantage can be taken of reasonable cooked meal prices.

Accommodation charges in high mtn. huts vary. 1977 average for dormitory = 80p. per night, for a bed in a room (mixed) = £1.25. These charges are raised 50% for non members of affiliated alpine clubs. Drinks, food and meals are the same price for everyone. In 1977 an evening meal of two courses = £2.00, add £1.75 for a litre of wine. Wine/drink prices are exactly double the cost of shop prices in valley resorts, but meal prices are only half as much again. Inn accommodation in the valley resorts = £3.00 bed and breakfast. In a 'C' category hotel = £4.50. A three course evening meal without wine = £2.50.

A tourist tax is added to all accommodation, meal and service charges in Yugoslavia (tipping is not required). For equivalent services and charges in Italy, add 50% to all Yugoslav prices.

CAMPING

There are authorised sites in both parts of the Julian Alps but they tend to be rather distant from the upper valleys. No official camping exists at Mojstrana, Kranjska gora or Trenta but there is a good site at the W end of Lake Bohinj below the Dom Savica roadhead. However tents and caravans are seen in fields in the upper valleys and one must presume that permissions are obtained. Local tourist offices, e.g. in Kranjska gora and Bovec, would give guidance on this matter. There is a picturesque campsite at the N end of the Lago del Predil (inn/restaurant) directly below the Italian side of the Predil pass; a convenient base for the West Julian mtns.

FOOTPATHS AND WAYMARKS

The Slovene Julians have one of the best marked footpath
systems in the Alps. Paths tend to be narrow but very good
underfoot and wayside trees and rocks are painted at frequent
intervals with a red circle round a large white dot alongside a
red number 1; this signifies a main walking route. Without
the figure 1, the route is of secondary importance - generally
not a traverse connection between hut stages. A few summit
routes have old waymarks and poor paths which have not been
repaired in recent times. Nearly all major ascent routes are
designated No. 1 and have fresh paint marks (1977). While
the occasional signpost appears in unexpected places, route
markings such as the names of huts, cols, summits, etc. with
directional arrows are written on trees, rock slabs and boulders at most important junctions or where doubt may arise as
to the correct continuation. In the Italian Julians a more con-
ventional system of paint flashes now mostly faint or erased
exists, while paths themselves can be followed in their vague
sections with the assistance of cairns.

Where the former frontier with Italy twisted through the
present Slovene Julians, several paths approaching strategic
points on this old frontier were constructed as broad mule
trails by the Italian military, e.g. Trenta - Luknja, Trenta -
Prehodavcih, etc.

Pass-crossings and approaches to summit ridges may follow
paths cut from solid rock. The most sensational and remarkable of these, like bits of the Jubilee Way and Bamberg Way,
are comparable with the most audacious via ferrata trails in
the Dolomites. Some of these 'iron routes' are too exposed
or strenuous for walkers and should only be undertaken by
climbers (indicated in guide).

22

SCOPE OF GUIDE

The work is intended primarily for mtn. walking and touring parties with experience of rough alpine terrain and familiarity with snowfields and snow slopes, and climbers interested in the ascent of principal peaks by routes up to grade III (see below). Difficult technical rock climbing above grade III is not described in any detail; a few indications of good routes are given. For further information on this subject one should consult the list of foreign guides at the end of this introductory section.

GRADING OF ROUTES AND CLIMBS

Several systems of grading for mtn. walking routes have been devised in Britain and abroad in recent years to distinguish from technical difficulties implied by mountaineering grades proper. This has led to some confusion and certainly a lot of inconsistency. In the present guide only the mountaineering rock climbing grades of I to VI in roman numerals are used, qualified for more accuracy by minus (-) and plus (+) signs; thus II-, II, II+ is the rising order through grade II. Absolutely safe paths for walking without particular steepness or hanging on to fixed ropes, etc. come into the lowest category, viz. I-. Level grade I will involve paths with steep loose sections (otherwise perfectly safe) on a high pass or mtn., rock scrambling pitches of no technical difficulty but a possibility of exposure at some points, and a certain amount of very secure artificial climbing with fixed ropes and iron rungs. At the level of II- there will be free rock climbing pitches equal to 'Moderately Difficult' in British rock climbing parlance. Above that, for instance, the middle of grade III is equal to the British 'Just Very Difficult' standard. Harder than that will be familiar to all those who so engage themselves with serious rock climbing.

MAPS

A locally produced road map of Slovenia in a scale of 1/300,000 is available from the Yugoslav tourist office in London (not sold commercially elsewhere in Britain). Code: AMZS 300m. Avtokarta Slovenije.

A map of a better cartographical standard with clear physical features and covering all the ground between Venice and Ljubljana is Code: KK 500m. Sheet 351, Tirol-Dolomiten-Vorarlberg. This series of maps in a scale of 250m. does not yet extend to the Julian Alps.

General walking/touring map of entire region: Code FB 100m. Sheet 14, Julische Alpen. Route descriptions in German on reverse side. This map is rather unsatisfactory - as are other large scale maps of the area - for detailed examination of the ground. It does however give a useful picture of the area and in several points of detail is more comprehensible than the PZS mapping (below).

Large scale maps: Modern Yugoslav mapping is poor by Alpine standards but there is no choice beyond the Italian map which only extends over the West Julians and N part of the East.

Code: PZS 20m. Julijske Alpe-Bohinj. First sheet of a new series published 1977. Only covers Lake Bohinj, Vogel chairlift area and lower part of Triglav Lakes valley, up to the lakes hut. Slightly better ground representation than PZS 50m.

Code: PZS 50m. Julijske Alpe, in two sheets East and West, divided at the Vršič pass. A comprehensive map, revised 1973. Contours are inaccurate and the delineation of rock masses is difficult to interpret. Best feature is the red overprint and numbering of paths which alone makes the map indispensible. Warning: the deployment and direction of paths on map are sometimes only approximate rather than inaccurate. Numerous errors in position and names of huts in W Julians area. Legend in English.

Code: IGM 50m. Italian ordnance survey grid sheets, all published 1964. A fairly good modern colour contoured map, of about the same standard as the British O.S. map, but not comparable with Swiss alpine maps or the French tourist series. Better than PZS, although clearly inaccurate in many points of detail.

Sheet 033, Tarvisio (Montasio, Fuart, Predil, Mangrt, key sheet for W Julians). Fits over top (N) of 050.
Sheet 034, M. Forno (Jalovec, Mojstrovka, Vršič, Prisojnik, Razor, Škrlatica, Špik, Kranjska gora, Mojstrana, Vrata). Fits alongside and E of 033.
Sheet 050, Monte Canin (M. Canin, Bovec, Kobarid, lower approaches to Trenta and Predil pass). Fits under (S) of 033.

Code: IGM 25m. Italian ordnance grid sheets. Does not cover as much ground as 50m. grid and extends only up to Yugoslav border. A good map, invaluable for W Julians. Minimum requirement as follows:

Sheet 14A III NO Cave del Predil
              NE Fusine in Valremana
              SO Sella Nevea
     14 II SE M. Canin
              SO Chiusaforte
              NO Dogna
              NE Jôf di Montasio

Code: ÖK 50m. Austrian ordnance grid sheet, no. 210, published 1969 (Triglav, Vrata, Mojstrana, Jesenice = Assling, S to Bohinj lake). While limited to the eastern approaches to Triglav, this map is clearer than all the others. There are no adjoining sheets.

All maps mentioned above are available from West Col Productions.

GUIDEBOOKS

<u>Tours and excursions to the Triglav mountains, the Julian Alps of Slovenia, Yugoslavia.</u> 39pp booklet issued for the year of international tourism. PZS, Ljubljana, 1967.

The undermentioned works are in Slovene, German or Italian.

<u>Triglav.</u> PZS, Ljubljana, 1968.

<u>Plezalni Vzponi-Vzhodne Julijske Alpe.</u> T. Banovec. PZS, Ljubljana, 1970. Definitive Slovene climbing guide.

<u>Die Slowenische Berg-Transversale.</u> PZS, Ljubljana, 1971.

<u>Julische Alpen.</u> H. Schöner. Rother, Munich, 4th ed. 1972.

<u>Escursioni nelle Alpi Giulie Orientali.</u> S. Gilić, P. Rossi. Tamari, Bologna, 1973.

<u>Alpi Guilie.</u> G. Buscaini. CAI/TCI, Milano, 1974. This last work is the most comprehensive publication ever attempted on the Julian Alps and is masterly in execution. However, the Slovene Julians are only a selection and a further defect is that the ground to the immediate S of Triglav, including Kanjavec, is (deliberately) omitted. Superb diagrams, photos and maps. Lire 12,750 in 1977.

GLOSSARY OF TERMS, FEATURES AND PLACE NAMES

Slovene	English
bel	white
bistrica	clear, bright
cesta	road
čez	upper
črno	black
desno	right (direction)
dolek	little (upper) valley
dolina	valley
dom	inn
glava	knoll, rock head
gola	ravine
goličica	naked summit
gora	mountain
gozda	woods, forest
greben	ridge
grlo	narrow constricted ravine
izvir	torrent
jezero	lake
jug	south
kačji	twisting, bending
koča	mtn. hut
konjsko	horse
konica	summit
kot	angular valley, also dièdre
kotel	hollow
kotli	hollow
krnica	cwm, cirque
lašta	series of small ledges
led	ice
levo	left (direction)
log	glade
mala, mali	little, small
mesto	rock pitch
most	bridge
možic	cairn
nevarno	dangerous
okno	window (in rock)
oprimek	hand/foot hold
ozebnik	couloir, gully
patoček	stream
peč	rock
pekel	hell
planika	edelweiss
planina	pasturage, alp
plezalni, plezati	climbing (technical)
plošča	slab

Slovene	English
pobočje	flank, side (of mtn.)
poč	crack
pod	lower
podi	valley bed, glaciated slabs
police	ledges
polje	field
pot	route path, trail
prag	brink - as on the edge of an exposed ledge
prečnica	traverse
prednji	outer
predvrh	forepeak
prelaz	pass, col
preval	pass, col
previs	overhang
prst	earth, finger rock
rama	shoulder
raz	buttress, pillar edge
rdeč	red
rob	edge, corner
rog	horn
rokav	sleeve, buttress
rumen	yellow
sedlo	saddle
sestop	descent
sever	north
severna stena	north face
skala	rock mass, buttress
škedenj	barn
skok	step (in slope or ridge)
škrbina	high pass, ridge gap
slap	waterfall
sleme	gable roof ridge
smer	route
sneg	snow
snežišče	snowfield
špiča	sharp peak
špranja	crack
srednji	central, middle
steber	pillar
stena	rock wall
stojišče	stance
stolp	tower
streha	roof
strme, strmo	steep
strmina	slope
suha	dry
suhi	balcony, access pt., view pt.
težko	difficult
tovorna pot	mule path

Slovene	English
trava	grass
veja	buttress
velik	great, large
visoki	high(er), upper
voda	water
vrata	gates
vratača	rustic
vratca, vratica	ridge gap, col
vrh	summit, peak
vršič	knoll-like eminence, apex, top
vrv	rope
vzhod	east
vzpon	ascent
zadnji	inner
zahod, zapad	west
zavetišče	hut
zelen	green
Zlatorog	In legend a white chamois with golden horns that kept watch over the magic gardens of the Rojenice at the S foot of Triglav
žleb	large open gully

Valley bases

YUGOSLAVIA

Soča - Trenta valley

Bovec (483m.) stands near the entrance to last stage of the Soča valley where it divides and turns almost due E; a N branch becomes the Koritnica valley giving access to the Predil pass. Shops, supermarket, garage, bank, post office, tourist bureau. Several hotels and inns. Campsite one km. from centre. Cableway in two stages to Prestreljenikom, just below frontier which further W carries M. Canin. A short walk E under then across the ridge at Prevala (2067m.) gives access to the Italian side and its chairlift system down to the Nevea pass. Bovec is therefore an excellent base for parties without their own transport wishing to go into the W Julians with loads and little effort. The cablelifts do not operate in poor weather or when demand is low. Then the long way round by bus up the Koritnica and over the Predil pass (1156m.) may be taken. Take care to ensure a good connection with another bus - only two a day - coming up the Val Rio del Lago to the Nevea pass.

A fairly frequent bus service operates from Bovec up the Soča valley which in its upper reaches becomes the Trenta valley, at the head of which is Vršič and a descent to Kranjska gora. This is the finest valley in the Julian Alps, cutting deeply through the mtns. and imparting tremendous scale to the flanking peaks.

Two km. from Bovec, junction of Koritnica and Soča valleys. A fairly narrow road with some potholes (not as good as the fine strada over the Predil) winds up easily to Kal Koritnica (hamlet) then Soča hamlet (inn, no shop). Starting point for a long but easy walking route SE over the Velika Vrata (1927m.) to huts in the Seven Lakes valley on S approaches to Triglav. Marked but not classified a No. 1 route. A lower pass to S leads directly to huts above the Dom Savica and Lake Bohinj area.

After Soča, in 40 min. motoring from Bovec, _Trenta_ village (622m.), formerly Na Logu (= in the glade), is reached. One food shop (limited opening hours), two hotels, and the Zlatorog mtn. inn. The latter is found one km. along road from village 'square', just round first sharp bend (junction with lane up Zadnjica valley), at a war memorial. Short-cut up a grass walk-way for pedestrians below this point. Buses stop at war memorial on request. 30 beds in 7 rooms, restaurant, bar, toilets, wash and shower rooms, terrace restaurant. Moderate rates. Carparking 100m. off road on greensward. Trenta is an important base for walking and climbing.

The valley road continues to rise more steeply, soon passing on your R an interesting chapel and the attractive botanical gardens of Alpinetum Juliana (small entrance charge) to reach a bend and junction with small road entering the Zadnja Trenta valley. One km. along this road is a small inn favoured by mtn. walkers, called the hut at the source of the Soča (876m.). About 16 beds, simple restaurant service. The river emerges gushing from a horizontal trench in the ground not far above the hut - a big tourist attraction.

The main road now launches into many zigzags to attain Vršič. At the first bend above the Source junction stands the statue/monument to Julius Kugy. The road is slightly wider, the gradient touches 1 in 7 in a few places and the surface is at present (1977) unmade except for good pavé on the bends. Vršič pass (1611m.) is reached in about 35 min. from Trenta. Three inn/huts on or near this pass are described in the Huts section. Carparking spaces along roadside but often crowded and blocked by tour coaches. Souvenir stalls; no drinks or meals for which you must go to one of the inns; no shop; no water! One of the most important junction of paths in the E Julians. Carefully note places on road where paths depart; the map is delightfully vague. The N side of Vršič is described under Kranjska gora (see below).

Bohinj Valley

This valley runs S then W from Bled to Lake Bohinj. Higher up it has a continuation to the N, above the rock barrier called Komarča, in the Seven Lakes valley of the Triglav national park. One of the most idyllic areas of the Julian Alps, and taken by thousands of walkers each year as a gradual route to the summit of Yugoslavia's highest mtn.

Bled (501m.) is a small town with a Riviera-like lake and beaches, a castle, camping and all main services. It lies a few km. off the main Ljubljana - Kranjska gora road. The railway comes in from Jesenice and goes up the valley to Bohinjska Bistrica where it enters a tunnel to emerge at Podbrdo, having left the district so to speak, and continues SW to Tolmin and Gorizia-Gorica. The road system into the Bohinj valley joined at Boh. Bistrica from Tolmin and Skofja Loka is not recommended. Between Podbrdo and Železniki it is very narrow and unmade, while the final section over the Bohinjsko sedlo (saddle) is alarmingly rough.

Good bus service on pleasant road from Bled to Boh. Bistrica, large village, and to E end of Lake Bohinj. At the Jezero Hotel and the church of Sv. Janez (St. John) junction N to Stara Fužina (546m. = old forge). in 2 km. Pleasant village with good amenities and starting point for SE side ascents of Triglav via a convenient hut system. The narrower main road follows the S shore of Lake Bohinj, campsite halfway along, to another campsite near the W end, below the Vogel chairlift. Buses go to the Zlatorog hotel, shop, now on a side road, while the rough main road follows the L edge of the valley to end at the

Savica inn (660m.), with the Savici hut nearby. Both do a
roaring trade with day-trippers. The mule path above, across
the L side of the Komarča barrier, leads to the hanging entrance
of the Seven Lakes valley (Komni hut); goods transporter cable
from Dom Savica. Trippers take a short R branch from this
path to the foot of the great wall from which pours the Savica
waterfall through a hole in the rocks. As advised in the Hut
routes part of the guidebook, adventurous mtn. walkers will
avoid the Dom Savica roadhead and use the Vogel chairlift to
follow the splendid high level traverse round the S edge of the
Bohinjsko basin to reach the Seven Lakes valley and its huts.

Pokljuka

A large forest area E of Triglav being progressively de-
veloped for winter sports. The new access road from Bled
(see above) via the Lower and Upper Gorje villages and by-
passing Krnica village is excellent to the first skilifts. Beyond
that it is very rough at present but wide enough and not unduly
steep; big potholes. It ascends to a junction where you go L
to the Sport Hotel (1250m., other inns close by) in 500m.;
this establishment looks like the London Hilton but offers accommodation down to dormitory sleeping. Keep straight on at
the junction through a barrier until military barracks are
reached at Rudno polje (1340m.). The barrier is closed when
conditions are bad for driving. The entire area is enclosed in
a huge forest - no views. On the ascent several side 'roads'
lead off into the forest; care must be taken at signposts. Past
the Sport Hotel it is possible to descend to the Bohinj valley
by a variable return route. Bus service: Bled - Sport Hotel.
Many further access developments can be expected in this
area.

This approach for Triglav has the merit of being one of the
quickest and easiest for those intent on arriving and leaving
quickly, and with no other plans in the area. A car is virtually

essential to achieve this, and 1050m. of ascent is involved from the Vodnikov hut to avoid staying a further night at the Planika hut not far from the summit (see main text).

Motorists should note that the little unmade road, occasionally rough, from Krnica (625m.) through the Radovna valley to Mojstrana is an excellent byway; it avoids the main road through Jesenice, harrowing at times. There is a short steep ascent and descent round the entrance to the Kot valley, otherwise easy with adequate signposts at junctions.

Krma and Kot valleys

Wooded valleys with a common entrance from Mojstrana, giving relatively lonely approaches into the central Triglav area. Very rough and steep unmade lanes partway - see next section of guide.

Sava Dolinka valley

The main road valley NW from Ljubljana to Italian and Austrian borders. Frequent train and bus services - bus only after the town of Jesenice (iron works) where the valley narrows a little. Very busy road carrying an immense amount of private and commercial traffic. In a few km. the road passes between Mojstrana and Dovje villages. Mojstrana (641m.) has come down in the world against the development of Kranjska gora but remains an important departure point, standing as it does at the entrance to the Vrata valley which leads directly to the N face of Triglav. All visiting parties will at some point want to make the journey up this valley. Mojstrana lives by this approach to the mtn. and its associations with Kugy's early climbs. Two hotels, an inn, post office and two/three shops. Climbers' bunkhouse and boarding houses across the main road in Dovje, the latter patronized by overnight-stop motorists. Mojstrana is a peaceful centre, disturbed only by youthful hordes passing through the village in cars and buses to invade

Vrata.

12 km. after Mojstrana the main road bypasses <u>Kranjska gora</u> (810m.), the Zermatt of the Julian Alps. This is a modernized and spotless village resort, quite the best in the region. If not ideally placed for all popular tours and climbs its position on the whole is a reasonable compromise for those who, with or without their own transport, prefer to have a comfortable base to return to on off-days. Good bus transport in all directions. About 8 hotels in category B and C, others a little way outside village, e.g. the popular Erika hotel, a few inns and boarding houses, shops of all kinds, 3 supermarkets, bars and restaurants, banks, post office, tourist/guides bureau, good taxi services, dancing and entertainment, tennis courts, all main services. Boating on lake in forest setting with magnificent backcloth of Škrlatica-Prisojnik.

The main approach into the mtns. is by the steep road up the Pišnica valley to Vršič pass (11 km., 40 min.). Like the approach from Trenta on the S side the road is fairly good but narrow up to the zigzag section. There it is a little wider but unmade at present except for pavé on sharp bends. Two gradients about 1 in 6. Various walks and climbs go off from points along the road, and in contrast to the Trenta side many pedestrians use the road. Four buses a day traverse the pass. For details of Vršič summit, see Soča-Trenta above.

At the end of the Sava valley, just short of Rateče village about 6 km. after Kranjska gora is the entrance to the Planica valley (see below) for Jalovec; shortly after this village the frontier crossing to Italy. Long hold-ups are possible at this border post at peak holiday times.

ITALY

Rio del Lago valley

At the bottom of this valley is the small town of Tarvisio (743m.), the next place of any size after entering Italy from Kranjska gora. From here two buses a day cross the <u>Nevea pass</u> (1190m.). The road is good all the way. Rather less than halfway up is the unattractive village of Cave del Predil (900m.), the last place supplies can be bought. Just above the fork L to the Predil pass and Bovec (excellent road) is car-parking, camping and an inn/restaurant at N end of lake (959m.) - a pretty spot, recommended. On the W side of the Nevea saddle, all in pleasant forest, are three hotels and the CAI Divisione hut (q. v.). Cableway in two stages to near the Prevala saddle (2067m.) on the frontier with Yugoslavia, directly above Bovec. Access lane to the Montasio upland plateau (see below).

The road on the W side of the pass descends with a few zig-zags easily to Chiusaforte in the Fella (Canale) valley, running S to Udine (ultimately Venice). The Canale road runs back N and E to Tarvisio, so marking the N boundary of the W Julians. At points along this road are entrances to the <u>Dogna valley</u> and <u>Valbruna</u> for access to the N side of the W Julians. Only a few notes are given in the guide for excursions on this side of the range.

Motorable mountain lanes

Zadnjica valley
1. From Trenta (Na Logu) leave main road on bend near entrance to Zlatorog inn. A narrow lane with few passing places, mostly at a moderate angle and one short section of 1 in 6. Halfway up (2 km.) greensward parking and unauthorised camping in forest at bottom of mule path to Pogačnikov hut. Water plentiful. Continue for another 2 km. to large level grassy glade in forest where road has barred sign for cars, 997m. Ample parking, unauthorised camping, water from stream (4 km. from Trenta, 15 min., $1\frac{1}{4}$ h. on foot). Steeper, rougher road continues through logging camp to become the No. 1 trail up the Korita to Luknja (pass) and Vrata on the N side; junction below the pass on this approach side to Tržaška (Dolič) hut - known as the Italian Mule Trail (q. v. Tržaška hut). No bus up this lane and no taxi service at Trenta. Generally busy with walkers in both directions.

Zadnja Trenta valley
2. From Trenta continue along the main road towards Vršič for 3 km. to the first prominent bend at the foot of the zigzags section. Turn L down a small road and in one km. reach a large open space where the small inn named after the Soča Source is found. This road continues in the flat valley bed, past the footpath on R (N) to Jalovec for a further 2 km. , petering out into a footpath.

Mangrtski valley
3. From Bovec drive the excellent road to within 2 km. of the top of the Predil pass (bus service). Just across the bridge

over the Mangrtski stream, at a large inlet in the mtn. slope, turn R (NE) at prominent signpost 'Mangrt' on to rough road-cum-lane (c. 1090m.). Approached from the Italian Rio del Lago side over the Predil pass, a shorter drive. About 45 min. from Bovec. No bus up the lane itself, taxi hire in Bovec. The lane continues for 11 km. to Mangrtu hut (q. v.) at 1995m., the highest road access point in the Julian Alps. Very narrow and rough with slithery bends and few passing places; about 5 sections in spiralling tunnels which are the easiest parts of the road. Turn L near top at signpost to reach hut; straight ahead it makes a short circuit above hut. Small parking area on a pasture well above the forest belt (30 min., 3 h. on foot from Predil road using after 2 km. a separate path in the forest; do not follow road on foot especially through tunnel sections).

Pokljuka forest road from Bled to Rudno polje

4. See Pokljuka entry in previous section. Fairly broad but very rutted. Roadworks improvement in hand during 1977. Bus service from Bled to Sport Hotel.

Krma valley

5. From Mojstrana follow the unmade road marked as leading to Radovna and Bled. It climbs fairly steeply at first to a R fork for the Kot valley. Keep L and descend keeping R at next junction to Bisček farm; this is roughest section. Ignore turning L (E) at farm for Bled and continue to next fork. Bear L to reach a T junction near Kurja vas farm. Now turn R and follow road into steepening Krma valley. This leads with a section of 1 in 7 to the Kovinarska hut (892m.), q. v. The road above hut peters out in a further 2 km. and is not advisable for cars. No bus service (45 min., $2\frac{3}{4}$ h. on foot).

Kot valley

6. From Mojstrana start as for previous rte. and fork R at first junction into Kot valley. The road soon becomes a steep and uncomfortable forest lane and runs up for another 4 km. Not recommended.

Vrata valley (Bistrica stream)

7. The busiest inner valley road in the Julian Alps. From Mojstrana follow the unmade road with quite a good surface at a moderate angle to the Peričniku inn. Fine spot opposite waterfall of same name. A little further reach a very steep 1 in 4 section with bends (25% warning sign) and above this a café on R. There follows a second 1 in 4 section (sign), somewhat rutted, to an upper easier angle; forested all the way up. Reach a magnificent glade dominated by the N face of Triglav, passing first on your R the annexe building to main hut, a chapel behind the carparking areas, then the enormous Aljažev hut itself (1015m.). Junction of broad forest paths with several groups of signposts. Restaurant and bar services, shop. See Huts section for further details. Bus service up and down valley from Mojstrana 5 times a day (11 km., 30 min., $2\frac{3}{4}$ h. on foot).

Krnica valley

8. A branch of the Pišnica above Kranjska gora. From latter resort follow main Vršič road for 2 km. to a fork L before the Erika hotel. Take the unmade narrow lane fairly close to the stream, rising steeply towards the end in a further 3 km. Small parking area (c. 980m.). This point is 40 min. walking distance from the Krnici hut, q.v. (20 min., $1\frac{1}{2}$ h. on foot).

Planica valley

9. A major rock climbing centre with some interest for walking parties. From the main Kranjska gora - Italian border road

turn L just before Rateče on to small road going up valley (signpost). Follow the straightforward unmade road with one steep section near the top to a large parking area beside the Planinski/Tamar hut, q. v. (6 km., 20 min., $1\frac{3}{4}$ h. on foot).

Fusine lakes valley

10. From Fusine hamlet on the main Tarvisio road take a lane over the railway and go up to the pretty Fusine lakes, upper lake (929m.) with official campsite beside an inn/restaurant. Continue by forest road for $1\frac{1}{2}$ km. to a junction and signpost. Do not take car beyond this point, which is about 1 h. walking below the Zacchi hut (5 km., 15 min., 1 h. on foot).

Riofreddo valley

11. A branch of the Rio del Lago with its entrance below Cave del Predil village. At the Riofreddo hamlet, just before the large bridge crossing (bend) on the way up to the Nevea col, turn R up a narrow lane between buildings. Follow this rough forest road to a chalet on the R (1041m.), then soon reach a twisting section. Leave the car here (1074m.), about 45 min. below the Calligaris biv. hut (5 km., 20 min., $1\frac{1}{2}$ h. on foot).

Grantagar lane for Corsi hut

12. Not marked on any map to date. Leaves the main Rio del Lago-Nevea pass road just above the normal footpath to hut at c. 1000m. This lane is forbidden to private motorists and in its upper section obliterates part of the hut track (q. v. Corsi hut).

Montasio altipiano

13. A rough unmade road leaves the Nevea saddle pass at the first bend after descending from top on the W side. Follow road for 4 km. with sharp uncomfortable bends and several

very steep sections of 1 in 5 to a junction. Continue L for the Pecol chalets (c. 1525m.), turn R for the Mezzo chalets (1552m.). Along the latter leave car at next little crossroads before Mezzo chalets to reach the Brazzà hut (q. v.) on foot. Mini-bus service two/three times a day (5 km., 20 min., $1\frac{3}{4}$ h. on foot).

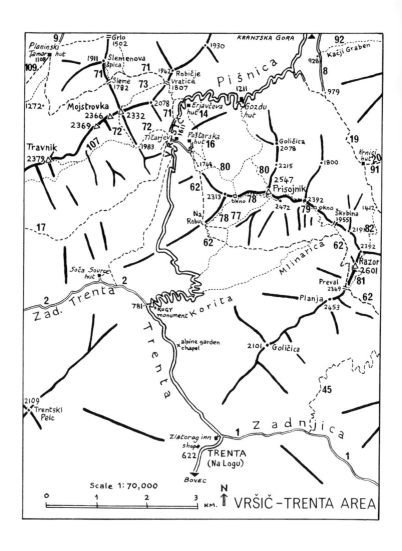

VRŠIČ–TRENTA AREA

Scale 1:70,000

Huts and other mountain bases

About 2/3rds of all establishments in the Julian Alps are included in this section. Some of the remainder are encountered in later descriptions while others are sited on ground not covered by the guide. High level links between huts are generally embodied in main routes though parts of hut routes may be repeated in the main sections to complete a traverse or a day's climbing.

VRŠIČ PASS AREA

Erjavčeva inn/hut   1515m.
14. Orig: Voss hut. Situated 500m. distance from top of pass, N side, on E side of road, along access drive. 70 places in dormitory and beds. Restaurant service, etc. Comfortable. Mostly used by family parties staying 3 or more days.

Tičarjev inn/hut   1620m.
15. From end of E side carpark just on S side of pass, 3 min. walk up jeep road to E. A large building much frequented by day-trippers. More expensive than other huts but more lavish in appointments. 100 places in dormitory and beds.

Poštarska hut   1725m.
16. Going up jeep road (private cars banned) past the Tičarjev, continue SE then round a sharp bend N to end of road in 15 min. The hut favoured by mtn. walkers and climbers. Good restaurant, etc. Comfortable. 60 places in dormitory and beds.

<u>Špiča hut</u> 2010m. (2040 over doorway)

Zavetišče pod Špičkom. Situated below S side of Jalovec and at foot of sharp peaklet of Vrh Zelenic (colloq. Špiča or Špička, 2278m.). A tiny hut with 12 places on mattresses, student warden in summer. No meals, only warm tea sold (not hot water). Barely 6-8 persons can sit at táble at one time. Self-cooking outside if desired. Cold water tap outside.

17. From Vršič pass (1611m.). Traverse Rte. 1. Gr. I-. Descend road S for a few m. past a souvenir stall on your R, to a short lane on R. Follow this for 2 min. to a fork. Take L branch and descend stony path under a smooth cliff. The path now climbs a little and commences a long up and down traverse above the Trenta valley, across forest and steep scrub slopes, easy going but effectively losing height. Eventually reach a water trough and a few min. later a closed chalet (c. 1580m.). A little beyond this the path forks 3 ways ($1\frac{1}{2}$ h.). Follow the middle way marked 'Špiča' and resume traversing to another junction (15 min.). Take the upper R branch and go up a series of rising traverses, getting narrow and quite steep in places. Enter the dwarf-pine zone and go up this on a rough trod to edge of the upper pasture (1 h.). Follow the good path with some steepness in easy zigzags towards a small sharp peak ahead (Jalovec well to R). Reach an old moraine and follow this to near the top; then bear L on to a grassy buttress at foot of Špiča and ascend in a few min. to hut (1 h., $3\frac{3}{4}$ h. from Vršič, 3 h. in descent).

18. From the Soča Source inn (876m.), adjoining S foot of Vršič pass. Gr. I-. A shorter rte. but generally recognised as more tiring. Nearly always used in descent. Good path. Continue down the Zad. Trenta valley to a water trough and signpost to R in $1\frac{1}{4}$ km. Go up the steep path N in zigzags past the Trenta alp chalet (1381m.) and in forest to a fork. Keep L and eventually reach the second junction mentioned in previous

rte., about 15 min. beyond the closed chalet ($1\frac{1}{4}$ h., $3\frac{1}{4}$ h. to hut; 2 h. in descent).

Soča Source inn   876m.
Koča pri izviru Soče. See Rte. 2.

Zlatorog inn   622m.
At Trenta village. See Valley Bases: Soča-Trenta section.

Krnici hut   1218m. (it appears to be c. 100m. less)
19. Situated in the broad wooded Krnica valley running up S to Razor, equidistant from Špik, Škrlatica and Prisojnik. Simple restaurant service, places for 25 in beds and dormitory.   Approach by Rte. 8 and pass a small lane returning across stream (928m.) to Vršič road. Continue by large path in forest to hut (2 h. all the way on foot from Kranjska gora, 30 min. from roadhead parking). Gr. I-.

Bivouac I   2180m.
Small aluminium shelter with 8 bunks. No warden. Key from Krnici hut warden. Located against N edge of the Vel. Dnina hanging valley among debris and snow patches, opposite foot of N face of Škrlatica. Free running water can be as much as 20 min. up cwm.

20.   From Krnici hut, Rte. 19, Gr. I. Follow waymarked level path E for Špik in woodland which gradually ascends the R side of Grunt o Vnica. Below the Grunt headland (1403m.) the path crosses the dry stream bed to continue NE up the L side of the bed for some distance before turning away L to mount scrub slopes.   Leave the path at this point and continue alongside the stream bed, trackless, getting into it and staying there until it rises into a big headslope cut by ribs and narrow stream courses below the Vel. Dnina cwm. Follow the main bed line to R and higher up get on to a rib of scrub and rocks to its L;

climb this tediously to the top. Trend a little L up the rocky cwm and ascend directly towards a small bay under the SW facet of Vel. Ponca, where the biv. is found ($2\frac{3}{4}$ h. from Krnici hut).

TRIGLAV - VRATA AREA

Aljažev inn/hut   1015m.
21. See Rte. 7. The largest establishment of its kind in the Julian Alps, and one of the largest in the entire Alps. Multiple dining rooms, bars, etc. , places for 180 in beds and dormitories. Annexe building for a further 70. Shop. Large relief map/diagram of Triglav N face routes on wall of building. Practice cliff for rock climbing fitted up with artificial aids, 5 min. away. Huge sculpture/memorial consisting of a piton and free-hanging karabiner set in a rock base dedicated to fallen wartime partisans, 7 min. away - "the most remarkable of all the world's war memorials" - R. W. Clark; another, more modest and in bronze, to fallen climbers nearby.

Bivouac IV   1980m. (but probably c. 2050m.)
An aluminium shelter with 6 bunks, water normally tapped into hut, wood for burning from scrub nearby. Door locked, key from Aljažev warden. Situated directly above Aljažev hut on the NW side of Vrata and on a little promontory in a pleasant situation.

22. From Aljažev hut. Gr. I-. Follow the trail E marked Škrlatica (signpost), at the start churned up by tractor tyres but watch out for tree markers. The track goes up steeply in a forest ravine and after 1 h. traverses L to reach a series of rock barriers above another ravine. It twists up these to exit R at the top among dwarf-pine and scrub. A rising traverse R (N) now leads to a fork returning L; go L to reach the hut

in a few min. (2½ h. from Aljažev hut).

Kovinarska hut   892m.
23. See Rte. 5. In the Krma valley above Mojstrana. Simple restaurant service, places for 30 in beds and dormitory.

Staničeva hut   2332m.
Dom Valentina Staniča pod Triglavom. One of a trio of huts in the vicinity of Triglav summit; well appointed, places for 95 in beds and dormitory. Situated on a broad saddle N of the Kredarica ridge and at the top of the Kot valley. A stage on one of the two main approaches to Triglav from Vrata, from where it may be reached by interchangeable rtes. The steeper, more direct and exposed is described while the other (Prag) is reserved for the Triglavski hut (see below).

24. Tominšek(ova) pot. Gr. I. Main rte. 1 waymarks. From Aljažev hut take the valley trail to the partisans' memorial, and just beyond (signpost) follow the L fork across stream. The gradually steepening path in beech forest enters a ravine and goes up the L side then the R to scrub (1331m.) and the edge of a big scree shelf. A rising traverse leads on to the Cmir rock walls where the height is marked every 100m. After a considerable direct ascent with several Gr. I moves on fixed ropes/pegs, exposed, and grand views of Triglav N face, the track makes a series of rising traverses R (S), some sections secured with aids, sometimes nicely exposed. Cross a big gully normally with snow in bed (stonefall possible) and continue under the walls of Begunjski vrh to emerge at c. 2000m. on a cliff edge where debris slopes rise towards the Triglav 'glacier'. In a few min. reach the junction of the Tominšek and Prag trails (4½ h.).

Just above is a concrete fountain under a rock, and 5 min. higher the trail divides. Take the L branch over rubble and snow patches to the saddle above and the hut (30 min., 5 h.

from Aljažev hut).

25. From roadhead in Kot valley (Rte. 6). Gr. I. The most direct way of all but depends on transport to roadhead. The track has old waymarks and is consistently steep in the upper cwm (Debeli Kamen) with a large snow bowl (Pekel) and a flight of slabs below the hut saddle (4 h. from roadhead).

26. From Kovinarska hut (Rtes. 5, 23) in Krma valley. Gr. I-. A long but easy rte. well marked up to the Polje plateaux but more difficult to follow after the Krma tarn, up debris/snow in the Travna Dolina. About 5 h. Not a logical rte. as one would go preferably to the Triglavski or Planika huts.

Triglavski hut   2515m.
The highest hut in Julian Alps, about $1\frac{1}{4}$ h. from summit of Triglav, situated at the W end of the Kredarica ridge and close to the foot of the E ridge of the summit pyramid. The usual approaches closely coincide with those of the Staničeva hut. Restaurant, etc., places for 130 in beds and dormitories. Meteorological station.

27. Pot čez Prag. Gr. I. Main Rte. 1 waymarks. See alternative way in Rte. 24, which is steeper and more interesting. This is the normal approach from Vrata to Triglav. From Aljažev hut take the valley trail past the partisans' memorial to a fork in 2 km., having passed a previous signpost to R. Bear L and cross the stream outlet gorge, sometimes awkward, and continue with snow patches round to a rock barrier under the N face of Triglav. Climb this (1374m.) with aids and pass L along a terrace to undergrowth which leads to a smooth rock nose, the Prag, 15m. high, climbed on fixtures. Continue the rising traverse L to another rock step called Pod Glava, and above this zigzag up a debris slope to some steep rocks below Begunjski vrh. In a few min. join the Tominšek trail coming

in from the L (Rte. 24), pass the concrete fountain and in 5 min. reach the upper junction ($4\frac{1}{2}$ h.).

Take the R branch and head S over debris and polished rock slabs of the kotel = smooth floor, towards the snowfield under Triglav. The track with snow patches gradually works up below the Kredarica ridge, then bears R along the upper edges of the snowfield, finally returning L to the hut saddle ($1\frac{1}{2}$ h. , 6 h. from Aljažev).

Staničeva - Triglavski hut connection

28. Gr. I. Either descend a little from former to follow a faint track over slabs and debris with snow patches under N side of the Kredarica ridge, to join Rte. 27 about 20 min. from Triglavski saddle (45 min.); or go under Rež (2535m.) and climb a short gully under pt. 2541m. (cables) to a ridge saddle then traverse the Kredarica ridge (2539m.) on broken rock by a well marked trail, keeping L (1 h.).

Note: Ways from Kot and Krma valleys. See comments in Rtes. 25, 26.

TRIGLAV - POKLJUKA, BLED, BOHINJ AREA

Vodnikov hut   1805m.
An intermediate stage on the gradual approach to Planika hut. Triglav is easily ascended without stopping at latter hut and early starters have been known to go up and down Triglav from Rudno polje in one day. Situated at the top of a depression dividing two grassy plains on the W side of Tošc (2275m.). Restaurant, comfortable, places for 55 in beds and dormitory.

29. From Rudno polje roadhead (1340m.), Rte. 4. Gr. I-. Waymarks. On the R (N) side of the barracks take a jeep lane (signpost) into forest, soon becoming a steep path rising W and working L round the Konjščica hill to pass above chalets

of same name (1438m.). Continue ascending steadily NE over grassland into another forest section at the top of which is a T junction in a grassy clearing called Jezerica, boxed in by the pastoral summits of Draški and Viševnik. Go L (SW) and ascend to the Studorski preval saddle (1892m.). On the other side the path commences a long traverse movement round Tošc, losing a little height among flowered slopes. In rounding the S corner of Tošc pass junctions of two paths arriving from below; then go under a rock barrier (1806m.) and keep R of a hillock Na zagonu (1824m.). Continue N over the Malo polje pasture to hut ($2\frac{1}{2}$ h.).

30. From the bridge in Stara Fužina (546m.). Gr. I-. Take the first lane leading N then L (NW) at a junction. Then on the R (signpost) a mulepath ascends the hillside above the Hudičev most (bridge), and goes up wooded slopes and meadows to the grassy trough of Blatca alp behind Studor. The path works N through several minor junctions and cross-paths and past chalets and sheds to the Uskovnica alp. On the R (E) is the large building of the Uskovnici hut (1138m.) ($1\frac{1}{2}$ h.). Restaurant, etc., pleasant location, 45 places in beds and dormitory.

Continue NW across the great pasture, ignoring a marked track on R (N) which goes to Konjščica alp (Rte. 29). After 2 km. enter the forest where the path twists up and down round the steep W slopes of Mesnova glava, then past Trstje alp and up to Tošc alp in a clearing. Now it makes a sharp turn SW over a stream gorge and circles round descending below Rte. 29 to join the latter on the S side of Tošc beside the descent under a rock barrier. Continue by Rte. 29 to hut (3 h., $4\frac{1}{2}$ h. from Stara Fužina).

31. From Stara Fužina a shorter rte. lies up the Voje valley, parallel and immediately W of Uskovnica alp, via Grintovica

alp (steep riser round cliffs) and the wooded clefts (Vrtača) of Jurjevčeva, to join Rtes. 29, 30 under the Na zagonu hillock about 20 min. from hut. In upper sections this path is narrow and tends to be overgrown ($3\frac{3}{4}$ h.).

Planika hut   2408m.
The hut closest to Triglav summit and the one invariably visited by parties coming from the Pokljuka and Lake Bohinj areas. Situated among scree mounds below the S side of the E ridge of the mtn. Restaurant, places for 65 in beds and dormitory.

32. From Vodnikov hut (Rtes. 29, 30, 31). Gr. I-. Waymarked. Take the prominent path N above the edge of the Velo polje grassland;   it works L then R on to the Konjsko saddle.   This broad col is a junction of several paths, care needed in poor visibility.   At the first fork running back L leave the saddle and follow the L branch over grass, scree and rubble in easy zigzags to the hut ($1\frac{1}{2}$ h.).

Note: By keeping straight ahead on the saddle and taking the next fork L, a steep scree/snow cwm can be ascended directly to the Triglavski hut (2 h.).

33. From the Tržaška hut. Gr. I-. Main rte. 1 markings. Ascend the big path behind building to the Dolič pass (2164m.) in a few min.   Avoid a R fork and descend directly, then go L (NE) under cliffs leading below Smarjetna glava to a grassy hollow which is contoured to below the S ridge of Rjavec. Climb and traverse round this ridge with ropes and rungs at exposed places, to stony slopes on the far side which are then ascended NE in zigzags to hut ($1\frac{3}{4}$ h.).

Planika - Triglavski hut connection
34. Gr. I. There is a rough marked trail round the rocky SE spur of Mali Triglav (2725m.) which makes two ascents and

descents.   Fixed ropes (1 h.).   Most parties will link the two
huts by first having gone up and partway down the Triglav summit pyramid (E ridge).

Savica/Savici huts   660m.
35.   For approach see Valley Bases, Bohinj section.   The
larger inn building has a restaurant and places for 30 in beds
and dormitory.   The nearby hut has only a bar and dormitory
sleeping.

Komni hut   1520m.
Situated in the lower forested approach to the Seven Lakes
valley above the Dom Savica roadhead.   Goods transporter
cableway on which rucksacks can be sent up for a small charge.
Restaurant, etc., places for 95 in beds and dormitories.

36.   Take the obvious large mule path W, climbing (turning on
R to reach impressive Savica waterfall of 60m.) in many zigzags up a large forest ramp between the Komarča rock wall
and another sub-wall below to a T junction at the top.   Turn L
to reach the hut in a few min. ($2\frac{1}{2}$ h.).

Bogatinom hut   1513m.
37.   Situated in a small forest clearing behind and to the NW
of the Komni hut, about 15 min. walk from the latter.   Restaurant, places for 55 in beds and dormitory.

38.   Much the best rte. for a high level touring party to enter
the Seven Lakes valley approach to Triglav, using the Komni
or Bogatinom huts as an overnight stop, is to traverse round
the Vogel-Komna (S) rim of the Bohinj basin.
    Gr. I-.   Waymarked but care needed to take correct continu-
ation at several junctions.   Above (S of) campsite at the W end
of Lake Bohinj, a side road for vehicles goes up in 300m. distance to the Vogel cableway station.   Take all the stages of

this to the top, cableway then two chairlifts, terminus at Vis. Orlov rob (1800m.). Join the path to L and follow it in 15 min. to the main ridge, a former Yugoslav-Italian border, at Sija (1880m.), rte. 1 markings. Continue W along the splendid ridge path with excellent views of Triglav massif to N, all the way. Descend to a col, then a lower depression (1668m.) before rising again to reach the top of Vogel (1922m.) in a circular movement L ($1\frac{1}{4}$ h. from cableway terminus).

The main trail now descends the other (S) side of Vogel to the Razor alp hut. Ignore this. Reverse the ascent rte. for 5 min. to a fork L (W). Follow a narrow rocky path under the N side of Vrh Krnic to a crossroads on the ridge at Globoko, 1828m., ruined shelter hut. Take the traverse path in same direction under N side of the ridge, soon ignoring a fork R, and wind in and out of gullies and round small spurs, losing a little height, before ascending again to the Konjsko saddle (1782m.). From here commences a regular descent N to the forest, passing a welcome spring soon after entering the trees. Eventually reach a crossroads at the Govnjač alp (1475m.). By continuing straight ahead (N) a path descends a little then rises in forest to the Bogatinom hut; by turning R (E) another path crosses a broad forest ridge to reach the Komni hut ($2\frac{1}{4}$ h., $3\frac{3}{4}$ h. to either hut from Vogel terminus).

Triglav Lakes hut   1683m.
Dom pri Triglavskih jezerih. The hut about halfway up the Seven Lakes valley, much visited as an overnight stage on the southern approaches to Triglav. Idyllic setting in open forest between 5th and 6th lakes (in descending order towards Komarča cliffs), and directly below the E-enclosing ridge of the valley. Restaurant, etc., places for 100 in beds and dormitories.

39. From Dom Savica roadhead (660m.), the shortest rte. Gr. I-. Waymarked. From just above the smaller Savici hut take a rough road on R across bridge (national park entry sign)

and follow this for 300m. distance to where the path proper starts its ascent to L (NW). Ascend steeply in wooded zig-zags to the foot of the enormous Komarča wall (a L branch goes along base of wall to the Savica waterfall). Now the path twists and slants up ledges and ramps in the wall for 300m. with artificial aids for assistance, to emerge at the top at pt. 1340m. on a large forest shelf. Turn L and in a few min. reach the 7th lake, Crno = black. Crossing above the N side the path continues through forest to a steep opening alongside a singular crag, Bela Skala = white. Zigzag up this section among dwarf-pine and scrub to a T junction on a large terrace under the E-enclosing ridge, where the forest thins out. Turn L through several glades and soon reach the shores of the 6th lake, Dvojno; on the N side of this the path from the Komni/ Bogatinom huts joins the present one and the hut stands a few min. away, just before the combined paths reach the 5th lake, Močivec (4 h.).

40. From Komni and Bogatinom huts. Both main rte. 1 way-marks. Gr. I-. From the latter return along the forest trail towards Dom Savica for a few min., then fork L along a big track in the forest, horizontal, which passes a junction on L arriving from the Bogatinom hut before coming to Razor alp. From the Bogatinom to latter junction, about 10 min. Now the trail winds N through forest without losing height. Pass a national park entry sign and turn a corner opposite the Bela skala crag (Rte. 39) to continue the forest traverse with more clearings in a big circuit to the E, S then E again, so reaching the ground on N side of Dvojno jezero where Rte. 39 is met a few min. from hut ($1\frac{3}{4}$ h.).

TRIGLAV - TRENTA AREA

Prehodavcih hut   2071m.

Zasavska koča na Prehodavcih.   Perched on a ridge below
Vršac, in a splendid position above the Trenta valley and right
at the top of the Seven Lakes valley. Often the limit for walkers
in the latter valley. Simple restaurant service, 25 dormitory
places.

41. From Triglav Lakes hut (1683m.), Rtes. 39, 40. Gr. I-.
Main rte. 1 markings. Leaving the hut follow path N past the
E side of the 5th Močivec lake along a picturesque floral trail,
under the Tičarica/Kopica ridge (below latter summit a L fork
goes off as a variant to traverse the W-enclosing ridge of the
valley over Malo Špičje). Proceed ahead N up scree past the
last trees in a few zigzags to the 4th lake, Veliko Črno = Big
black (1830m.) and follow its E bank to a resumption of steep
scree with large fallen blocks scattered round; so reach the
3rd lake, Zeleno = green (1998m.). At this lake ignore prominent turning up steep track to R and follow waymarks horizontally N to 2nd lake, Rjava Mlaka = Brown pool (2002m.). Just
after this another fork R (ignore). Continue towards the skyline
ridge, passing between a tarn on your R, called Laštah, and
a smaller pool to L. Now ascend gradually over scree above
the last (1st) lake, Podstrenju = cliff bottom, to where the
track turns L below a saddle and continues mounting briefly
to hut ($2\frac{1}{4}$ h.).

42. From Trenta valley, two ways to the Čez Dol saddle
(1632m.). The first is proper on foot, the second is shorter
by driving to the Zadnjica roadhead. Both Gr. I-, ropes, etc.
on sections above saddle but only because this military way
has become dilapidated. Main rte. 1 markings on first approach.

  (I) From Trenta (Na Logu, 622m.) walk down main road

for one km. to prominent signpost to hut on L up a meandering cart-track serving farms. Follow this into a mule path entering the forest under Krotica alp (955m.), taking R side of Trebiški valley then L side to Lepoća and Trebiščina alps, above an impressive gorge. The path eventually bends N at an easier gradient to arrive at the Čez Dol saddle (1632m.) ($2\frac{3}{4}$ h.).

(II) Above Trenta, at the Zadnjica valley roadhead, Rte. 1 (997m.). Follow the jeep road for a few min. to a small track on R. This crosses ledges over two rockbands in a rising traverse S to climb loose rock slope into the Zadnjiški valley running up deeply enclosed to SW, which is followed steeply all the way to Čez Dol saddle ($1\frac{3}{4}$ h.).

From the saddle the mule path winds up rock terraces below Zad. Lopa to a long upward traverse L, culminating in more zigzags to the ridge above. Descend L on the Seven Lakes side to hut ($1\frac{1}{2}$ h., $4\frac{1}{4}$ h. by Trebiški valley, $3\frac{1}{4}$ h. by Zadnjiški valley).

Tržaška hut   2152m.
Called by everyone 'Dolič hut'. Situated just below the Dolič saddle (2164m.), the main ridge depression between Triglav and Kanjavec, and facing the Trenta valley. A notable 'flog up' from latter but no worse than many in the district, on a path called the Italian mule trail that could not be much better. Simple restaurant service, places for 50 in beds and dormitory.

43. From Trenta (Na Logu, 622m.). Rte. 1 markings, Gr. I-. Follow Rte. 1 to Zadnjica roadhead (997m.). From here continue up the jeep road through lumber camp, bearing L at all junctions into a regular-mounting mule trail in forest - seemingly endless zigzags above the Korita ravine, to a junction at c. 1530m. Straight ahead, the Luknja (pass) to Vrata. Turn R (E then S), signpost, and climb with progressive steepness

in and out of shallow ravines to reach large scree bands and ramps stretching below the smooth terraces of Triglavski podi, often snow covered in July. Continue without much relief in the angle to a final series of zigzags leading to the hut (3 h. from roadhead).

44. From Prehodavcih hut (2071m.), Rtes. 41, 42. There are two ways; the second is only recommended to persons with mountaineering experience.

(I) Gr. I-. Waymarked. Descend Rte. 41 to the 3rd lake, Zeleno (1998m.), and go up a steep stony track (signpost) to L which at the top enters a scree cwm called Hribarice on the S side of Kanjavec. Among the rocks continue easily E, passing a L fork to Kanjavec, and reach the Čez Hribarice saddle (2358m.), also a junction for another way up Kanjavec. The saddle is a superb viewpoint. Now take the path N, descending wide scree fans and snow tongues under the Kanjavec cliffs and finally traversing to the Dolič saddle (2164m.). The hut is immediately below on N side ($2\frac{1}{4}$ h.).

Note: There is a short cut into the Hribarice cwm, starting from a L fork just before (N of) the Rjava Mlaka tarn; it looks steeper than the usual way.

(II) Direct rte. across N side of Kanjavec. An airy marked trail with genuine Gr. I+ movements without fixed ropes, and several sections with aids in place. From the hut descend the approach path for a couple of min. to a big bend and there take a small track ahead (NE) over craggy steps in a steep ascent to the Vršac saddle. From here descend with some exposure on loose rock in a large groove to a terrace running R (facing out) which traverses high above the Zadnjica valley. It progressively narrows and crosses gullies and ribs where hard snow/ice may be found. An ascent section leads round a big buttress, exposed, to the upper zigzags of Rte. 43, which is reached some 15 min. below hut ($1\frac{3}{4}$ h.).

Note:

From Triglav Lakes hut (1683m.). The same as Rte. 41 to Zeleno lake, where Rte. 44 (I) is joined and followed (4 h. to Tržaška hut).

From Planika hut (2408m.) reverse Rte. 33 ($1\frac{1}{2}$ h.).

From Vodnikov hut (1805m.) by steep stony trail and snow-fields W up the Velska valley to Dolič saddle (3 h.).

Pogačnikov hut   2052m.

Situated on the last grassy knoll in entrance to the wild and stony Kriški cwm between Razor and the Stenar group. One of the most visited huts involving a stiff walk in the district. A stage on one of the most strenuous and technically most difficult high level scrambling rtes. to Triglav, which commences at Vršič. Restaurant, comfortable, places for 75 in beds and dormitories.

45. From Trenta (Na Logu, 622m.). Gr. I-, waymarked. Go up the Zadnjica valley (Rte. 1) for 2 km. to small clearing on bend with carparking and signpost for hut on L (N). Follow a good mule path all the way, at first in a long forest section, then on the other (R) side of the stream draining the Kriški cwm, up many zigzags into the dwarf-pine zone and terraced rock bands with constant steepness to a large platform from where the hut is reached by a track to L ($3\frac{3}{4}$ h. from Trenta main road, save 30 min. with car).

Pogačnikov - Aljažev huts connection

46. Gr. I-, main rte. 1 waymarks. From the Pogačnikov hut take the good path E over honeycomb limestone and hollows to an ascent bending L (N) up scree to the Sovatna pass (2180m.) (40 min.). On the other side descend a steep gully and rough slopes in the Sovatna cwm, and down through narrows to the Bukovlje forest below (two sections with cables). A steep short cut goes off L down the N edge of the forest, but the usual and

now gentle trail branches R (SW) to join the Luknja path just below its bad screes. Continue down the Luknja path below Triglav N face into Vrata and so by level walking in the valley to Aljažev hut (2 h., $2\frac{3}{4}$ h. from hut to hut, $4\frac{1}{4}$ h. in reverse direction).

Pogačnikov - Tržaška huts connection

47. Gr. I-, main rte. 1 waymarks. Start as for Rte. 46 and reach the Sovatna pass. Turn R (S) and go along the ridge towards Bovški Gamsovec, first on the crest then R of it along ledges with fixed ropes to a steep pitch (rope) leading to crest again and a little col below the summit; the top can be reached in 5 min. by easy rock. Descend L (S) down a series of narrow terraces with cables above a steep wall into a shallow scree cwm. Follow L side of hollow, under the ridge running down to the col below and so reach the Luknja pass (1758m.) ($1\frac{3}{4}$ h.). Go down Trenta side of the pass to the junction in Korita with Rte. 43, and follow this to Tržaška hut ($2\frac{1}{2}$ h., $4\frac{1}{4}$ h. from hut to hut; same time in reverse direction).

CENTRAL JULIANS AREA

Planinski/Tamar hut   1108m.

48. One of the most important rock climbing centres in the East/Central Julians, situated in the Planica valley above Rateče (main road from Kranjska gora). See Rte. 9. Full restaurant service, etc., places for 70 in beds and dormitory.

Mangrtu hut   1995m.

49. Situated at the roadhead pasture NW of Mangrt, one of the great viewpoints of the Julian Alps. See Rte. 3. Restaurant, places for 30 in beds and dormitory.

<u>Canin - Prestreljenik cableway</u>   c. 2200m.

50. Upper terminus situated 15 min. below and S of a saddle
called Škrbina pod Prestreljenikom (2282m.) in the ridge descending ESE from Prestreljenik on the frontier, some distance
E from M. Canin. Important starting point for frontier crossing into W Julians. The absence of any direct rte. to M. Canin
from Yugoslav side at present (hut destroyed by fire) allows
the cableway to be used to reach Italian approaches to Canin
quite easily, via the Gilberti hut (see below). Restaurant at
terminus, no accommodation.

From Bovec by waymarked trail to W of cableway, 4 h.
Small road to c. 800m. and continuation suitable for jeeps only
to c. 1200m. Cableway journey takes 20 min., lower station
one km. down main road from centre.

<u>Divisione Julia hut</u>   1162m.

A large hotel-like building on W side of Nevea pass in Italy,
on S side of road, reached by driveway. Nearby inn and hotel
and lower station of Canin cableway. A good base for Canin
group and W Julians. Restaurant, etc., places for 80 in beds
and dormitory. See Valley Bases, Rio del Lago valley section.

51. From top of Prestreljenik cableway on Yugoslav side, by
a large well marked path. Ascend this behind terminus buildings over scree and possibly snow to the Škrbina pod Prestreljenikom (col, 2282m.), then traverse descending slightly NE
round small hollows and spurs under the frontier ridge to a
short zigzag ascent NW to the Prevala frontier saddle (2067m.).
On the other side go down in a few min. to upper chairlift
section of the Italian cableway system (1 h.). From col to
Gilberti hut on foot by marked trail generally with snowfields
where rte. is variable, 30 min. From col all the way down to
Nevea pass and Divisione hut, $1\frac{1}{4}$ h. on foot.

Gilberti hut   1850m.

The main hut for M. Canin, on Italian (N) side of mtn., above the Nevea pass. Situated below and SE of the rockhead called Bila peč. Restaurant, 55 places in beds and dormitory.

52.   From the Nevea pass and Divisione hut (see above). Gr. I-. Take a waymarked mule path from L (E) side of cableway station. At first this has been churned up by ski tows and runs which can be followed until the original path develops on R. Continue past the Nevea chalets to zigzags near the cableway, then cross below latter to R side, and follow up the overhead cables closely to below terminus of the first stage. Then traverse R to zigzags below the cliffs of Bila peč and at the top reach hut on the L ($2\frac{1}{4}$ h.). By using first stage of cableway, take a track directly up to hut (15 min.).

From top of cableway on Bovec (Yugoslav) side, see Rte. 51.

WEST JULIANS AREA

Corsi hut   1874m.

Base for the Jôf Fuart group above the Rio del Lago valley, situated SE of the main summit. Restaurant, 50 places in bunks.

53.   From the Nevea col road at pt. 984, where the road crosses the Torto stream coming down from direction of hut. Some 50m. further up road an unmarked track rises into the forest. Follow this with waymarks appearing at intervals until it joins a rough road (forbidden to cars) coming in from L. Continue along road with short cuts over the original track until the road must be followed all the way to Grantagar alp. Below these chalets and further R continue under a transporter cable and go up a mule path in zigzags, due N to the hut on a large grassy terrace ($2\frac{3}{4}$ h. from road).

Brazzà hut   1660m.

54. Base for the Jôf di Montasio group above the Nevea pass, situated on the extensive grassy slope called Altipiano del Montasio, close to mini-bus terminus (Rte. 13). Simple restaurant service, 15 dormitory places. From the last crossroads before the Mezzo chalets (1552m.), or from chalets themselves, follow marked paths to N and reach hut in 15 min. ($2\frac{1}{4}$ h. on foot all the way from Nevea col).

Grego hut   1389m.

55. Base for N side of the Jôf di Montasio group. Restaurant, etc., with 45 beds. Reached from roadhead in Valbruna (Malga Saisera, 1004m.) in 45 min. Or from roadhead in Val Dogna (Sella di Somdogna, 1397m.) in 15 min. The Stuparich biv. hut (1587m.) is an advance starting point above the hut, directly below NE side of the Montasio.

Mazzeni bivouac   1630m.

56. On the N side of the W Julians, situated at the bottom of the upper Spragna cwm, ringed by savage rock peaks forming the great loop of towers and summits between Montasio and Fuart. 9 bunks, door open. Simple walk of 2 h. or so from Valbruna roadhead (Malga Saisera, 1004m.) by a waymarked path.

Pellarini hut   1499m.

57. Base for N side of the Jôf Fuart group. Restaurant, 40 places. Easily approached from Valbruna village (807m.), by small road and mule path in $2\frac{1}{2}$ h. Road section is driveable for 1 h. of this time.

Triglav - ordinary and high level routes

TRIGLAV   2863m.

Ger: Terglou, Terglau. Ital: Tricorno. Latin: Mons Tullus.
The highest mtn. in Yugoslavia. The summit area is a fairly
regular pyramid of three ridges standing on a truncated dome
so that snowfields and snow/scree terraces (the Ger. word
'band' is appropriate) encompass it. The N side is cut away
in an elongated precipice nearly 3 km. wide and 1000m. high
above the Vrata valley - far and away the most outstanding
feature of the range which brought the region to the attention
of outsiders. Two of the three summit ridges are normally
followed and both are equipped artificially. In its pristine
state the E ridge would be Gr. II. The N ridge running back
from the top of the N face is sometimes taken as a finish to N
face rtes., and is also a more dramatic finish to the Bamberg
Way. A small emergency shelter carved out of rock is found
just below summit on E ridge. Also beside summit is the
small red metal Aljažev tower intended as a storm shelter.
The name Triglav signifies 3 heads, so called not because the
mtn. has 3 summits - with Mali (Little) Triglav as a mere
shoulder on E ridge it has barely 2 - but attributed to an
ancient Slav deity who had 3 heads.
     First ascent: Lukas Korošek, Matija Kos, Štefan Rožic,
Lorenz Willonitzer, 26 August, 1778. In winter: J. Kugy and
party, 26 December, 1899.

East Ridge. The most frequented rte. for the final ascent.
Every section with any pretence to technical difficulty is safe-
guarded by cables, rungs and steps hewn in the rock. Nevertheless an impressive little ridge. Gr. I.

58. From Triglavski hut (2515m.), or Staničeva hut (2332m.).
See Rtes. 21, 24, 25, 26, 27, and Staničeva-Triglavski connection, 28. Main rte. 1 waymarks.

     From Triglavski hut go down in a couple of min. to a saddle
and on the far side work up a rock strewn slope to a little spur
which is climbed on its L side with cut steps and stanchions
to a junction with path coming up from the Planika hut.

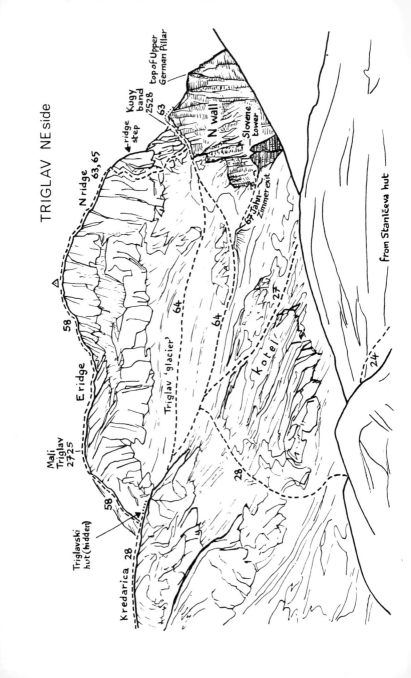

TRIGLAV NE side

top of Upper German Pillar

Kugy band 2528

ridge step

N ridge 63, 65

N wall

Slovene tower

69 Jahn-Zimmer exit

E ridge

64

64

27

Triglav 'glacier'

Kotel

58

Mali Triglav 2725

28

24

Triglavski hut (hidden)

58

Kredarica 28

from Staničeva hut

Continue more steeply for a few min. to top of the shoulder/ spur, <u>Mali Triglav</u> (2725m.). Now the ridge becomes horizontal, sharp and exposed. Pass along it with fixed cables and cut footholds, past a memorial plaque to the first of two short rock steps. Go up this to another plaque and climb the second step to a point just R of the artificial rock cave. In a few more steps the summit ($1\frac{1}{4}$ h.).

59. From Planika hut (2408m.), reached from Vodnikov direction by Rtes. 29, 30, 31, 32; from Tržaška direction by Rtes. 33, 39, 41, 44. Main rte. 1 waymarks.

From the rear of hut take a waymarked trail N over rubble and usually snow patches to traverse R to rocks under Mali Triglav. Climb a short rockband then the track rises L to ridge above where Rte. 58 (q. v.) is joined not far below top of Mali Triglav (1 h. to summit).

<u>South Ridge (from Triglavska/Bovška škrbina)</u>. Called Čez Nogo - a reference to Julius Kugy; first ascent by his party in 1881. A more sporting but in fact less interesting way to the summit. This ridge also concludes the Bamberg Way along WNW ridge from Luknja. Gr. I, waymarked.

60. From Planika hut follow track up narrow cwm W, under S side of Triglav, debris and normally large snow beds, to a steep broken rock slope below the col. Climb this by a complicated rte. on loose shelves and ramps, some of them tottering, where concentration is needed to locate the waymarks; cut steps and cables in place. Reach Trig. škrbina, a narrow col at foot of ridge (2659m.). Follow the ridge keeping to R side of crest on shattered rock up to a short steeper rib leading directly to summit ($1\frac{3}{4}$ h.).

61. From Tržaška hut, direct. Rte. 1 waymarks. Gr. I. A little below hut a mule path forks R from the descent to Trenta.

TRIGLAV SE side

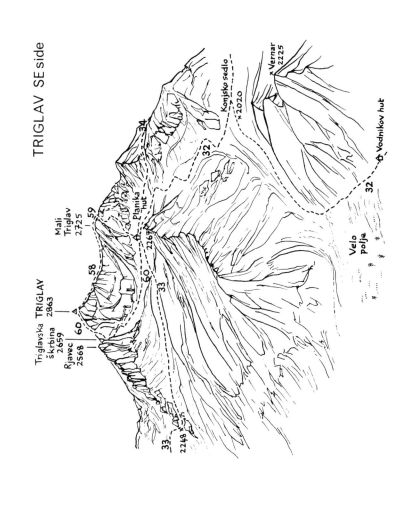

Triglavska škrbina 2659

Rjavec 2568

TRIGLAV 2863

60

58

59

Mali Triglav 2725

Planika hut

2263

34

60

33

32

Konjsko sedlo
×2020

Vernar 2225

32

Velo Polje

Vodnikov hut

33

33

2248

It takes a high level undulating line N along the top of the Trig-lavski podi slab terraces; zigzags in ascent and descent, finally passing R at a junction above the ruins of former Italian barracks to reach a junction on debris slopes where the Bamberg Way arrives from the Luknja pass. Turn R up rubble and usually a large snowfield, steepening up to a rock wall under the Trig. škrbina. This is cut by a gully, reached from the L by ascending a red ramp with fixed cables. Climb the moderately steep gully bed to the ridge gap where Rte. 60 is joined ($2\frac{3}{4}$ h. to summit).

Vršič High Level Route. The classic modern approach to Triglav, normally two days, but followed less frequently than the 2-day N side approaches from Vrata. The appeal is two variations that can be taken on the first day, to include Prisojnik and/or Razor in the expedition. Including both makes for a very long first day, not less than 12 h. These diversions apart the second day becomes the longer, over the Sovatna pass, down to Luknja then up the Bamberg Way. The first day variations are described under their respective mtn. headings.

Gr. I from Vršič to the Luknja pass. Bamberg Way, I+, and its variation finish by the Kugyband and N ridge, II-, for climbers only. At the Luknja pass walking parties should continue to the Tržaška hut by Rte. 47, and go from there to the summit by Rte. 61 - the tactics recommended locally for leisurely-going parties. Rte. 1 waymarks on all sections except the Bamberg Way, where clear paint flashes are in evidence.

62. First day, from Poštarska hut (1725m.) (Rte. 16), above Vršič, to Pogačnikov hut (2052m.).

Return along jeep road for 5 min. to a large concrete bunker and pass this on the L. Ahead, several small tracks run up a dwarf-pine ridge to a knoll (Savna glava, 1748m.). Take one just below crest on R side; this contours round knoll across

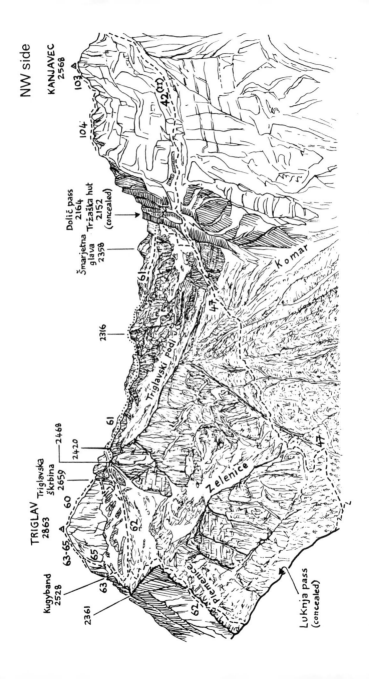

NW side

KANJAVEC
2568

103

42 (77)

104

Dolič pass
2164
Tržaška hut
2152 (concealed)

Šmarjetna
glava
2358

Komar

61

47

2316

Triglavski Podi

2469

2420

61

TRIGLAV
2863

Triglavska
škrbina

60 — 2659

63-65

65

Zelenice

62

47

Kugyband
2528

63

2361

62

Planica

Luknja pass
(concealed)

a gritty gully to a small saddle on far side. At large boulders turn R and follow a rising traverse path S over scree, at the far side mounting more steeply into brush-covered slopes by short zigzags to reach a corner/shoulder called Na Robu (1820m.), where the path turns due E. At the first level spot on this shoulder is a small fork L marked Prisojnik; in a few paces further a wooden signpost on R (50 min.). Turn R and descend a narrow track in zigzags, easing after 10 min. but losing height all the while towards denser forest below. Pass a junction on L marked (again) Prisojnik and follow the descending path until it commences an up and down traverse for some distance high above the Korita valley (Mlinarica). Some short slabs and shallow gullies are crossed with water by the wayside. Eventually reach grassy slopes in the upper part of Korita. A series of zigzags leads to moraine above, which is followed to a prominent crossroads with signpost, etc., not far below the enclosing pinnacled ridge ($1\frac{3}{4}$ h.).

Take a moraine track SE crossing normally two wide snowbeds in a traverse to reach the upper L side base of the huge rock wall under Razor. The transition from snow to rock can be delicate. Go up debris covered terraces rising L to R, getting on to the highest one as soon as possible where a good track follows below the wall up to a small shoulder. Descend a big rock ramp on large polished holds for 50m. to a level continuation. In a few min. reach another little shoulder. Turn sharp L up a short pitch, then go under a large overhang to a continuation ramp rising from R to L. The first pitch of this has a fixed cable, then a walking angle above. At the top of this enormous ramp the track in rocks goes R then L to a small shoulder above the main rock wall. Continue by an excellent path in scree, making a long rising traverse movement R, usually with several snowbeds, under the S ridge of Razor, to reach the splendid col of Preval (2349m.) between Razor and Planja ($1\frac{1}{4}$ h., about 4 h. from Vršič).

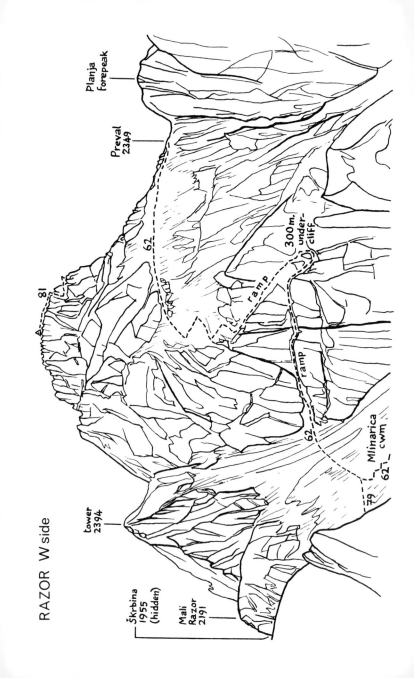

RAZOR W side

Planja forepeak

Preval 2349

81

62

Škrbina 1955 (hidden)

Mali Razor 2191

tower 2394

300 m. under-cliff

ramp

ramp

62

62

Mlinarica cwm

79

On the other (S) side descend steep variable tracks somewhat R in scree and snow into a small cwm. The Pogačnikov hut can be seen all the way. The track crosses smooth slabs on L (cable) and descends a steep pitch on iron rungs to more scree, following the base of cliffs to L, along broad ledges to a junction. Straight ahead the path dips through two small hollows and rises onto the grassy headland where the hut is situated (1 h., 5 h. from Vršič. Same time in reverse direction).

Second day. From the Pogačnikov hut take a good path E over rocky terrain and hollows at the S edge of the Kriški podi cwm to an ascent bearing L (N) up scree to the Sovatna pass (2180m.) (40 min.). Turn R (S) and go along the ridge towards Bovški Gamsovec (2389m.), first on the crest then R of it along ledges with cables to a steep pitch with a chimney (cable) returning to crest again and a little col below the summit; the top can be reached in 5 min. by easy rock. Descend L (S) down a series of narrow terraces with cables above a steep wall into a shallow scree cwm. Follow L side of the hollow, under the ridge running down to the col below and so reach the Luknja pass (1758m.) ($1\frac{3}{4}$ h.).

Above the pass follow painted rock markers of the Bamberg Way (A. Bois de Chesne, 1892) on to the steep, vegetated lower WNW ridge of Triglav. Slightly on the R side of the crest this gives continuous and interesting scrambling with several Gr. I/ I+ sections without cables on three successive steps, returning L at the top where the angle eases. Now follow the ridge crest to the L of a zone of terraces called Plemenice, along the top of part of the tremendous N wall until the track moves R on to scree and snow slopes. Junction with variation L (Rte. 63) to Kugyband. Keep R and go up debris hillocks and snowbeds to the junction with Rte. 61 a short way below Triglavska škrbina. Follow latter rte. and S ridge to summit ($2\frac{3}{4}$ h., about $5\frac{1}{4}$ h. from Pogačnikov hut).

Note: From Aljažev hut in Vrata to Luknja pass, then up Bamberg Way to Triglav as described above, about 5 h.

63. Variation finish to Rte. 62, by the <u>Kugyband</u> and N ridge. Gr. II-. J. Kugy, 1882. From the junction indicated in Rte. 62 follow a vague track near the edge of the N wall, slightly upwards over rubble and slabs due E, probably snowy. After 15 min. reach the apex opening to the Kugy ledge, at the highest point (2528m.) on the N wall where broken rock ribs descend from a step supporting the N ridge above. The ledge slopes progressively downwards and outwards at an angle of 20°. Follow it, possibly delicate due to snow/ice conditions, and contour a little rib then another near the bottom to a scree/snow cone (15 min.). Straight ahead this ground opens out into a hollowed slope below the N ridge, and offers a fairly steep traverse on to Triglav 'glacier'. Climb directly above the end of the ledge on the last rib descending from the L edge of the rock step below N ridge. Steep broken ground leads to the slabby side of the ridge which is taken on loose rock to the crest above the step (old waymarks). Continue along the ridge, turning small obstacles with little difficulty, to summit ($1\frac{1}{4}$ h., $1\frac{3}{4}$ h. from junction on Bamberg Way).

64. To reach Triglavski hut from end of Kugyband, thus E ridge of mtn. Continue across fairly steep rubble and snow, either making a slightly rising traverse above a hollow, or contour below a few outcrops about 50m. distance away from edge of N wall. Either way move directly over the Triglav 'glacier' due E to reach the saddle ahead and hut (30-45 min. from end of ledge).

65. Original finish to Bamberg Way. Before reaching the foot of rock ribs supporting N ridge (Rte. 63), and before upper end of Kugyband, bear R up a scree/snow slope to the rocks on R of step. In the upper corner the ridge flank is cut by a

snow/rock gully. Climb this (II) for 70m. to broken terraced walls, then to the ridge above and continue along crest to summit (1¼ h. from junction on Bamberg Way).

LUKNJA   1758m.

Little Hole pass.   The most important pedestrian col in the vicinity of Triglav, traversed by a military mule trail and leading from Trenta (Na Logu) to Vrata (Aljažev hut).   Most of the ground on both sides is described in previous rtes. Main rte. 1 waymarks.   Gr. I-.   On the Vrata side the upper section takes a steep debris couloir where the track is rough then over scree until it improves under the Bukovlje woodland and down to the Prag junction.   From Zadnjica valley road-head to pass, 2 h.   Same time from Aljažev hut.   In descent, about 1¼ h. both sides.

TRIGLAV NORTH WALL

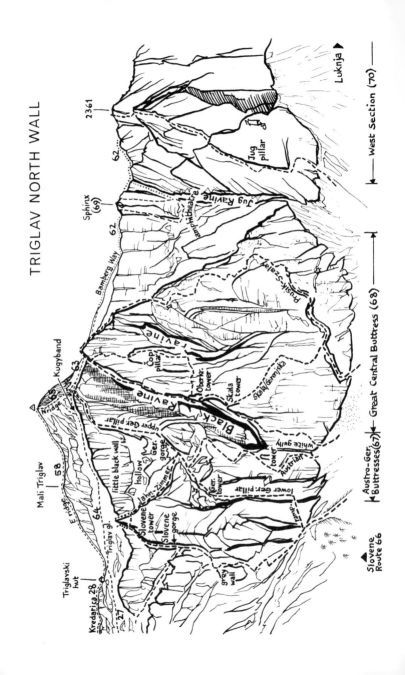

Luknja ▶

West Section (70)

Austro-Ger. | Great Central Buttress (68)
Buttresses (67) |

2361

62

Jug pillar

Sphinx (69)

62

Bamberg Way

amphitheatre

Jug Ravine

Rusk-Szalc

Mali Triglav 58

E ridge

Kugyband

N ridge

63

63

Black Ravine

Čop pillar

Oberkr. tower

Skala tower

Skala/Gornjiska

Triglavski hut

Kredarica 28

27

Triglav 9.

64

upper Ger. pillar

little black wall

hollow

Ger. gorge

Kahn-Zimmer-
Slovene tower

Slovene gorge

Ger. tower

lower Ger. pillar

tower

Austrian

white gully

grey wall

Slovene
Route 66

Triglav north wall

This great rock wall, one of the highest and most extensive in the Eastern Alps, stretches for nearly 3 km. from the Luknja pass (W) to the large diagonal break under Begunjski vrh (E) taken by the Prag (Rte. 27). The apex of the wall is somewhat L of centre where it reaches a height of 1200m. above the inner cwm of Vrata. In a vertical line this point co-incides with the upper end of the Kugyband and the base of the summit pyramid which is marked by the terminal N ridge (Rtes. 63, 64, 65). Therefore the total vertical interval from base to summit is in the region of 1500m. and is equal to the longest climbing rtes. anywhere in the Alps.

The R-hand (W) section is detached from the main part by the great gash of the Jug Ravine. The W section rises some 700m. to pt. 2361m. on the WNW ridge followed by the Bamberg Way; it diminishes further R to merge into the Luknja pass.

The main part of the wall is cut by the huge Black (Central) Ravine directly below the Kugyband, fading into grooved white walls before reaching the bottom. R of this is the outstanding Great Central Buttress reaching up the full height of the face, itself cut from top to nearly bottom by another ravine twisting R-wards. The dividing Jug Ravine to the W has above an amphitheatre an impressive recessed upper wall, marked by a large pillar called the Sphinx.

L of the Black Ravine a series of complicated buttresses is cut by another big ravine (the German gorge) and associated pillar edges and smaller gullies. The distinct pillars provide the main climbing lines and the intermediate gullies tend to be avoided nowadays; the exception is at the L side where the

Slovene Rte. makes its way. Across all parts of the wall, roughly at mid-height, runs a series of complicated and partly disconnected ledges and ramps, called the Zlatorog ledges, which give a grandiose girdle traverse.

About 20 rtes. have been made on the wall, and many variations. Rtes. climbed today tend to be a combination of several original lines. Route finding everywhere on the wall is the main problem. The rock is generally good where it is steep but otherwise tends to be brittle; it improves from L to R across the face. Stonefall is not a particular problem although debris litters ledges and ramps. Low angled rock and easy ground on the more popular rtes. have small tracks worn in them. A brief outline of worthwhile rtes. is given below, from L to R across the wall.

<u>Slovene Route.</u> The easiest way up the wall, at its L side. Climbed frequently. Several variations are possible in the lower part and there are at least three exits through the Slovene gorge in the upper part. Mainly Gr. II with pitches of III. Probably climbed by hunters in late 19th century. First recorded ascent: Dr. H. Tuma with J. Komac, 21 August, 1910.

66. From Aljažev hut start as for Rte. 27 and follow waymarked trail to the terrace traverse L above the first rock barrier with cables. Just before this traverse reaches a scree gully rising above, leave the trail and ascend directly by a vegetated buttress, narrowing up to the base of the wall between (normally) two large snow patches. A gully cuts the wall above ($1\frac{1}{2}$ h.).

The easiest way up the first section is to move diagonally L up a chimney/ramp line for 100m. to below a group of larch trees higher on the face. Move R along a ledge and from near its end climb back L up a ramp and easy rock to the larches. From just below the larches follow ledges and small steps diagonally R to a conspicuous zone of grey rock (there are more direct ways to this point), some 250m. above foot of wall ($1\frac{1}{2}$ h.). Climb the R side of the grey wall using an open chimney system to a little ridge at the top. Cross L to a small hollow and from it exit L up a steep pitch (III) to an obvious traverse line running R for 30m. into a gully. Climb this on broken rock for two rope lengths until it is possible to move R into the huge Slovene gorge, normally with a fairly steep snowbed ($1\frac{1}{4}$ h.). Follow the bed for 80m. to a long rubble filled gully cutting diagonally L in the E wall. Climb this to the top of the wall in a further 150m. ($1\frac{1}{4}$ h., 4 h. from foot of wall).

A better exit from the gorge follows the bed to near its top, below steep rocks and a big headwall. Climb an initial chimney line on the R of a waterfall, then traverse R along a narrow ledge (III) to cross the ridge of the Slovene Tower on the R. Continue traversing R to reach a scree/snow hollow under the terminal headwall (called Little Black Wall) on R-hand side of Slovene Tower summit. Ascend diagonally L to exit at top of wall without actually touching tower again.

An alternative takes the wet chimney line above the back of the gorge, keeping R, and finishes up terraced walls to summit of Slovene Tower. These variations add at least $1\frac{1}{2}$ h. to the total climbing time compared with the normal exit.

67. <u>Austro-German Buttresses</u>. The extensive area of rock between the Slovene gorge and tower (E) and the Black (Central) Ravine (W) has a complicated structure. A big depression marked by the German gorge cuts the upper part; above this lies an elongated hollow overlooked by a headwall (Little Black Wall). The upper buttress dividing the German gorge and Black Ravine is the continuation German pillar or Long German Rte. Its lower part fades into a narrow buttress/wall called the Austrian Rte. or tower. Below and L of the German gorge, the L side of this entire area is called the original German

77

pillar which is deemed to terminate in the German tower about
halfway up the wall - although it has a continuation right up to
the headwall hollow. (The narrow pillar/buttress further L,
not strictly part of this general area, is capped by the Slovene
tower).

Various ways up this massive buttress give some of the
longest climbs on the wall, up to 1200m., with crux pitches
by any combination at Gr. IV+. The more popular combinations
consist of parts of older rtes. linked with newer ones to provide worthwhile expeditions. By the easiest start (original
L-hand German rte.) the first ascent of this area was made by
K. Domeigg, F. König, H. Reinl, 3-4 July, 1906. The most
direct line, starting on the R, was first done in 1926 (Austrian
tower rte.). The Jahn-Zimmer exit (4 August, 1906) is the
shortest escape from the wall, passing L under the R side of
the Slovene tower; it has one pitch of IV+. The more direct
finish by the Long German rte, or upper pillar, is slightly
easier but longer and more sustained (IV). Both are climbed
frequently. The latter finish combined with the Austrian rte.
start (IV+, fairly sustained) gives the finest combination. Many
other combinations are possible. Route finding is complicated
throughout and the rock is generally good where it matters on
key pitches.

The foot of the buttresses is best reached by descending
along the base of the wall from the start of the Slovene rte.
($1\frac{3}{4}$ h.). By Austrian and Long German rtes. combination,
13 h. to Kugyband. By lower German pillar and upper (Long
Rte.) pillar, 8 h. to Kugyband. The latter with Jahn-Zimmer
exit, 6 h. Austrian and Jahn-Zimmer combination, 10 h.

68. <u>Great Central Buttress</u>. The magnificent triangular rock
mass, the largest independent area of rock on the wall, bordered on the L by the Black Ravine and on the R by the Jug
Ravine. Somewhat R of its apex the area is cut by a huge ravine

which peters out some distance from the bottom. A conspicuous pillar marking the L side of the ravine from halfway up
the wall is the Čop pillar. The L-hand ridge continuously
bordering the Black Ravine is the finest pillar edge anywhere
on the N wall of Triglav. One third way up, the Skala tower;
halfway up, the Oberkrainer tower; the latter is level with
the base of the Čop pillar to R. Below the Black Ravine the
ridge fades into steep walls of white rock adjoining the Austrian
rte. on the Austro-German buttresses.

Nearly all logical climbing lines are combinations of rtes.
done individually over three decades. Straight up the walls
below the L-hand pillar ridge and continuation by the ridge past
the Skala and Oberkrainer towers = 1200m., generally IV+
with pitches of V+, A2. Above the Skala tower the climbing is
mainly IV with one pitch V. The very difficult wall start to
the ridge is normally avoided by commencing with the Skala/
Gorenjska combination, which reaches the Skala tower by a
complicated but fine rte. from the R (IV/V-). The Čop pillar
is reached from the Oberkrainer tower by a horizontal traverse
R of 150m. (IV), and the climb itself is V+, A1. All these
rtes./combinations are rated among the finest of their class
in the Eastern Alps. Average climbing time 15 h. Rock generally good.

The R-hand side of the buttress is taken by the Prusik-Szalay
rte., about 1200m., IV with a pitch of V.

69. Jug Ravine/Amphitheatre. Divides the Great Central
Buttress and W section of the wall. Whereas the amphitheatre
can be reached from the bottom up the ravine by a Gr. III rte.
it is subject to stonefall, and the great recessed wall of the
Sphinx above the amphitheatre is normally approached by descending from the Bamberg Way at the top, in a couloir (II).
An alternative approach is by the Prusik-Szalay rte., from
which a complicated traverse R leads into the amphitheatre.

The headwall is dominated by the vertical Sphinx pillar, 250m. high, with rtes. of VI, A3, dating since 1960.

A broad ridge defines the R side of the Jug Ravine and marks the L side of the W section of the wall. This ridge is the Jug pillar, one of the best and most straightforward climbs in the area, 850m., IV with two pitches of V.

70. <u>West Section of North Wall</u>. Bordered by the Jug Pillar on the L (see above). Several rtes. approaching 700m., but diminishing to less than 400m. at the R side, have been made in this section, which is noted for its good rock. Generally IV/V.

East Julian summits

SLEMENOVA ŠPIČA   1911m.

Popularly called Sleme, one of the prettiest walks in the region.
Return the same way. Gr. I-. Waymarks.

71. From Vršič pass (1611m.), at the highest point of the
road take a footpath N through bushes to a series of short zigzags (junction with variation path coming from N side of pass)
in scree leading fairly steeply to Vratica, col (1807m.), 30
min. Splendid views. Junction with Mojstrovka rte. Continue straight ahead, round a little hollow and descend slightly
along a broad rib of rocks and trees. Cross rib to R side and
traverse forest high above the Mala Pišnica valley, passing a
junction on R for descent to Planinski/Tamar hut. Ascend a
little under the large grassy promontory of Slemenova špiča
and bear away slightly L over grass to a surprising col, Slatnica (1782m.) (40 min.), where a tremendous vista of Jalovec
and the Travnik-Šita walls round the head of the Planica valley
unfolds. From col a small track descends to Planinski hut, an
interesting excursion. However, for an even better viewpoint
follow a vague track from col up the grassy ridge NNW to the
top of the špiča (20 min., $1\frac{1}{2}$ h. from Vršič, $1\frac{1}{4}$ h. in reverse).
   Note: walkers are not recommended to use the alternative
track from Vratica (Rte. 73) which contours scree/boulder
hollows under Mojstrovka to reach Slatnica by a slightly shorter
rte. Less pleasant, rough and several snow slopes.

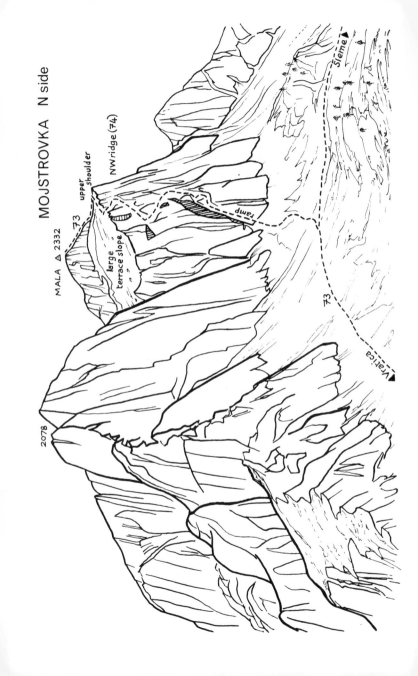

MOJSTROVKA N side

MALA △ 2332

73

upper shoulder

NW ridge (74)

large terrace slope

ramp

2078

73

Vratica

Sleme

MOJSTROVKA   2369m.

A bulky mtn. of flattish profile and of considerable interest;
climbed frequently.   It has three summits along the ridge
leading away SW from above Vršič pass: the Mala (2332m.),
Velika (2366m.) and Zadnja (2369m.).   Most parties only go
to the Mala. The NW side of the trio, facing the Planica valley,
commences one of the most majestic rock walls in the Julian
Alps, 5 km. in breadth and over 800m. high across Travnik
and Šita. First ascent, probably in 18th century. Mojstrovka =
Master mtn.

<u>South-East Side.</u> A first class outing, excellent views, highly
recommended. Gr. I-. Waymarks.

72. From Vršič, opposite long carparking space on S side of
pass, a small grassy hollow appears below roadside. Take a
track in bushes and open forest contouring above the R (N) side
of this hollow, soon reaching with a few short zigzags scrub
then scree under the SE ridge of the mtn. In a rising traverse
go up to the ridge on broken rock, to a little saddle (1983m.).
On the other side a short descent, then follow up the track
under ridge and gradually bear L over the rough ground called
Grebenec, directly below S side of the Mala summit.   Go
straight up to the top over debris and broken slabs where much
of the original path has been destroyed by erosion (1$\frac{3}{4}$ h.).

<u>North Side Route.</u> A rock climb rendered amenable by cables
and large pegs.   An excellent rte. for making a simple traverse of the Mala. Gr. I, steep, exposed, waymarks.

73. From Vršič follow Rte. 71 to Vratica (1807m.), junction.
Turn L (SW) and follow a small track rising easily over scree/
snow slopes falling from the NE ridge cliffs. In 10 min. cross
a broad shoulder, beyond which the track levels out then descends.   On levelling out, leave it for a vague track rising L
on scree then snow, fairly steep at the top, to below the gully/
depression dividing the rock mass overhead (pt. 2078m.) from
the main rock mass further R. At the bottom of the depression

stands a rectangular detached buttress. To its R a great ramp slants R across the cliff face, below an elongated overhang in the same direction. Reach the foot of the ramp (50 min.) and climb it for 75m. with cables, etc., then traverse a gully and on the far side climb a steep exposed corner to a line of shallow chimneys, exiting L over short steps. Continue trending L towards a black stratified overhang, and within 20m. of this turn sharp R below terminal overhanging rock. Just past the overhangs exit trending L up ledges and short walls to easy slabs forming the cliff top. The track follows up near the cliff edge to the fine upper shoulder of scree and snow. Keep slightly R of the shoulder crest line and climb the summit pyramid ridge on good rock in a nice position (2 h., about 3 h. from Vršič).

74. <u>Other North Side Routes.</u> R of Rte. 73 the cliffs below the upper shoulder have at least two climbs of Gr. IV, but the best and most popular rock climb is the short NW ridge, marking the R-hand edge of the zone, above a gap at the top of a snow couloir. A fine little rte. of 250m., IV.

75. <u>North-West Face.</u> This develops under the Velika and Zadnja tops as two or three large, square-cut buttresses, rtes. from 400 to 600m., IV to VI. Rarely done compared with the bigger climbs on Travnik further R.

<u>Mala-Velika-Zadnja Summit Ridge.</u> Small rough track difficult to find in the rocks. Gr. I-.

76. From the Mala top descend for 5 min. by Rte. 72, then traverse SW to rejoin the summit ridge above a short steep riser. Follow the ridge on broken rock to the Velika top (15 min.). Continue along the absolutely flat ridge with a precipice on the R (N) side to the Zadnja summit (15 min., 30 min. from Mala). Return same way.

PRISOJNIK 2547m.

Ital: M. Prisani. Ger: Prisang, Prisank = Sun-basked mtn.
An elephantine rock mass, tilted roof-like on S side, and sculptured by terraces, hollows and complicated flying buttresses
across immense N face cliffs. Noted for its okno = window
rtes., huge holes in the main W-E ridge. Proximity to Vršič
pass ensures it becomes one of the most frequented summits
in the region. A traverse in combination with Razor is the
most classic 'non climbing' expedition in the East Julians, not
excepting any combination on Triglav. First ascent, probably
hunters in early 19th century.

<u>South-West Side by South Gully.</u> The easiest rte., a bit tedious
and better in descent. Gr.I. Rte.1 waymarks.

77. From Vršič/Poštarska hut, follow Rte.62 to Na Robu
(1820m.). Continue past wooden signpost on R, along a traverse path over grassy slopes under SW side of mtn. In 20
min. reach a small junction with a direct descent track marked
'Razor' ($1\frac{1}{4}$ h.). Bear L up grass to short zigzags and enter
the wide S gully opening. Steep grass and rocks in bed, then
movements on R side to boulders in the upper bed. Here a
section on snow might be delicate, then by steep pleasant rocks
on R side to reach a shoulder above gully, at the top of a fine
buttress. A good track follows upper rib of buttress to another
fine vantage point in the summit line. Make a rising traverse
L over the Prisojnik roof on a wide scree path to reach the
last V gap L (W) of the summit. Traverse R, soon about 50m.
below ridge, over broken slabs to reach the upper end of a
track in scree coming up from a lower level. Follow this in
a few min. to summit ($1\frac{1}{2}$ h., $2\frac{3}{4}$ h. from Poštarska hut).

<u>West Ridge Window.</u> One of the best scrambles of its class
in the region. Gr.I+. The slab pitch above window is Gr.II
but has a sound fixed cable. Rte.1 waymarks.

78. As for Rte.62 to Na Robu (1820m.). A few moments before the wooden signpost take a steep little track L in dwarf

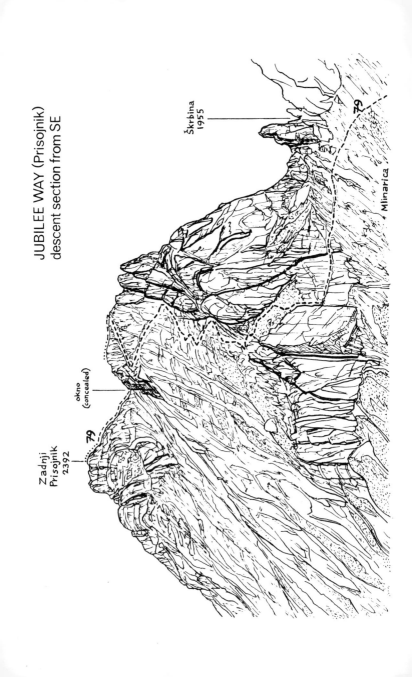

JUBILEE WAY (Prisojnik)
descent section from SE

Zadnji
Prisojnik
2392

79

okno
(concealed)

Škrbina
1955

79

Mlinarica

pine, winding up the SW ridge of pt. 2313m. or 2348m. Emerge on steep grass just R of crest and go up trending R into a depression in the white cliffs above. Climb pleasant steepening rocks, with a short traverse L at one point which is not obvious, to finish suddenly on the brink of the lower lip of the great window making a hole some 30m. wide and 80m. deep under the W ridge ($1\frac{3}{4}$ h.). Move R up pleasant rock near a little ridge further R and reach the broad W ridge, steep at first with short rock steps; when in doubt move R round obstacles. Reach a smooth slab just R of crest and ascend it with fixed cable (10m.) to exit on scree and broken rock. The track goes L of crest then R, crossing small ridge gaps and false summits, in general keeping slightly R, to reach the last ridge gap before summit where Rte. 77 is joined and followed to top ($1\frac{1}{4}$ h., 3 h. from Poštarska hut).

East Ridge Window (Jubilee Way). Trail equipped in 1953 to mark 60th anniversary of Slovene Alpine Club. Invariably used in descent by parties traversing to Razor and Pogačnikov hut. A fine rte., Gr. II in its pristine state, waymarks faded in 1977. More exposed and several steeper pitches than Rte. 78. Path is literally hewn from solid rock over considerable stretches. Experienced mtn. scramblers only. Gr. I+ with bits of II (cables and pegs). First ascent, 1906.

79. From the summit descend by Rte. 77 for a couple of min., then take a lower track in scree below the slabs traverse, still working (illogically) W. Just before track appears to finish, and well before V gap in ridge is reached by Rte. 77, descend directly L down the Prisojnik roof by delicate low-angled slabs for 30m. (cable). Next bear L (facing out) and follow small track in a slightly descending traverse E across roof to join the E ridge. The path cannot be lost now. Descend broken rock below L (N) side of ridge, under the Zvoniki rock head (2472m.), and by ledges and a short reascent gain Zadnji

PRISOJNIK NW face

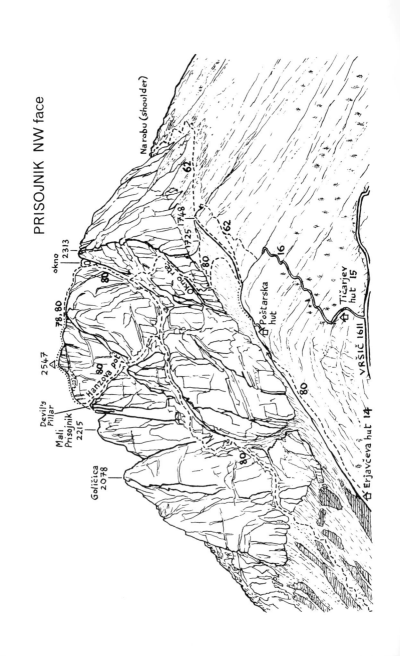

Goličica 2078

Mali Prisojnik 2215

Devil's Pillar

2547

Hanzova pot

okno 2313

78,80

Narobu (shoulder)

62

748

725

veliko okno

80

62

Poštarska hut

16

Tičarjev hut 15

VRŠIČ 1611

80

Erjavčeva hut 14

Prisojnik (2376m.). Follow down steep pinnacled rocks near crest (cables) and pass below a huge vertically-cut window 20m. high. Gradually leaving the crest zone, the track now makes a series of impressive descending traverses divided by steep pitches in short chimney/couloirs in S flank of ridge. The lower steps are near vertical, to work round a rock spur and wall extending E below it. A final ledge traverse over a gully brings the track to within a short distance of the narrow Škrbina col (1955m.), marked by a large pinnacle. Cross grass slopes horizontally below pinnacled ridge to reach the prominent crossroads of paths in the Mlinarica cwm, under Razor, Rte. 62 ($1\frac{1}{4}$ h. from summit). From here by Rte. 62 to Pogačnikov hut/Razor, or return to Vršič.

80. North Face Routes. This complex wall is divided into two parts by a massive spur jutting N from the summit area into the Pišnica valley, and is marked by the subsidiary towers of Mali Prisojnik (2215m.) and Goličica (2078m.). A smaller spur juts NNE from Zad. Prisojnik towards the Krnici hut. Between the two rises a relatively enclosed and short (500m.) wall of ribs and couloirs. The NE face of Zad. Prisojnik is clean cut and has important climbs of 700m., III to V. The main interest however centres on the NW face formed between the N spur and W ridge of the summit proper - facing the Vršič road. This face is climbed by two equipped trails, for climbers only, the most serious of their kind in the East Julians; and a good technical rte. called the Devil's Pillar.

The R-hand side of the face is taken by the Okno rte., the start of which can be seen and reached from the Poštarska hut in 30-40 min. It follows up steep rockbands L of the W ridge into a mini-cwm which funnels up to exit through the window of Rte. 78. Gr. II, allowing for cables, etc. in place; very exposed. $4\frac{1}{4}$ h. to summit.

The L-hand or Hanza pot rte. is even more varied and

properly commences under the R side of the N spur. It too is well marked and equipped with aids for a height of 1000m., traversing R across the base of the Devil's pillar into the middle of the face before returning L steeply up snow and rock ramps to the top of the pillar, to finish up the last step of the N spur directly under the summit. Gr. II free climbing. $5\frac{1}{2}$ h. to summit. This rte. can also be reached by a marked traverse L from the Okno rte.

The Devil's Pillar, mostly just R of the front edge then L of it in the upper third, is c. 400m., IV+ (Baebler, Zupančič, 1936).

RAZOR   2601m.

A chaotic rock pile of regular outline, not a climber's mtn. but a favourite expedition for scramblers. The rock is rather poor. Razor = furrowed ridge. First ascent: O. Sendtner, about 1842.

South Side. Virtually all ascents are made by this rte., either from the Pogačnikov hut (shortest by far), or from Vršič (quite long). Ideally 'bagged' in the course of passing between these two points by Rte. 62. Gr. I, no artificial aids. Steep snow plaques possible. Waymarks.

81.   From the Preval pass (2349m.), reached by Rte. 62 ($1\frac{1}{2}$ h. from Pogačnikov, 4 h. from Vršič) follow a small track over debris under S ridge of mtn. The track skirts terraces under R side of ridge, beside (normally) snow slopes to R again. Further up it steepens on loose scree/snow, making a short zag L and R over two little terraces before mounting a short open gully to reach a little saddle at the top; the E shoulder. Go back a few paces to a terrace running L across the S face, rising gradually below steep buttressed rocks, and at the far end go right round a corner on to the W side. Almost immediately climb a little chimney/couloir (snow possible) to reach

the summit ridge and follow this on crest to top. Some 80m. away is another top of about the same height along a shattered crest (45 min. from col, 25 min. in descent).

North-East Face.   Above the Krnica valley, a direct way to summit from Kranjska gora. The original rte. by Kugy (1888) takes the L side to the E shoulder, a poor climb on loose rock, Gr. II.   The Jug rte. outlined below is better, with 700m. of scrambling and climbing on rock, snow or ice. Gr. III. K. Jug and party, 1924.

82.   From the Krnici hut (1218m.) follow the waymarked Kriška stena (pass) path up the wooded valley to scrubland below moraine.   Move R over scree to the foot of the Razor wall (c. 1500m.) and go up its L base normally in a big snowfilled groove bordered by an old moraine.   Start about 150m. up this groove where a depression cuts R in the rocks above ($1\frac{1}{2}$ h.).   Climb steeply R over grassy ledges, broken slabs and ramps to a shoulder almost directly above the lowest point of the face. (This shoulder can be reached by steeper climbing from near the lowest point below).   Continue straight up and slightly L in a narrow depression to a ramp slanting L and giving access to a long sinuous gully slanting L across the middle and upper parts of the face.   Follow it for 250m. with alternate sections on rock, debris and snow/ice.   Exit on to a triangular snowfield (from where a relatively easy escape can be made L to the E shoulder of Rte. 81).   Climb trending R to the head of the snowfield, then take a series of gullies in steep steps, trending L to a notch in the E ridge from where the summit is soon reached (about 4 h. , $5\frac{1}{2}$ h. from Krnici hut).

KRIŽ   2410m.

83.   A secondary summit (= Cross) between Razor and Stenar, frequented from the Pogačnikov hut.   By the SE ridge along

exposed waymarked trail with cables, etc., Gr. I+ ($1\frac{1}{4}$ h.).
First ascent: G. Kugy with A. & J. Komac, 1897.

STENAR   2501m.

Stonewall.   An independent bastion jutting E from Križ and
separated from it by the deep gap of Stenarska vratca (2295m.).
An impressive NE wall overlooks Vrata.   Climbed often.

From South-West.   The usual rte. by which most ascents are
made.   Waymarks.   Gr. I-.

84.   From the Pogačnikov hut take a good path E over rocky
terrain and hollows at the S edge of the Kriški podi cwm to an
ascent bearing L (N) up scree to the Sovatna pass (2180m.)
(40 min.).   Turn L (N) and follow L side of ridge to a rock
wall running R.   Move R below this, passing under the Stenarska vratca and ascending snow to a spur of debris further
R (E).   Follow a discontinuous track up this spur to the top
(50 min., $1\frac{1}{2}$ h. from hut).

85.   North-East Face.   Has several rtes. from 350m. to 650m.,
III to VI approached from Aljažev hut in $1\frac{1}{2}$ h.

PIHAVEC   2414m.

Windy mtn.   A continuation of Bovški Gamsovec (2389m.),
Rte. 62.   One of the most difficult rock peaks (III+) in the E
Julians.   No marked or equipped trail from Pogačnikov hut.

o

Note: Jalovec is very much a Vršič area summit but this mtn.
merits an area description of its own (q. v.).

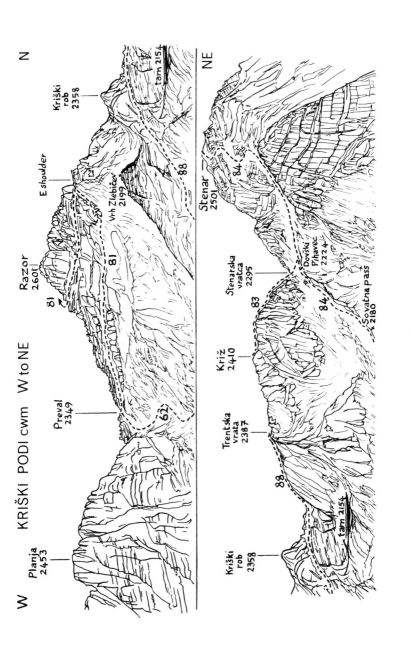

KRIŠKI PODI cwm   W to NE

W

Planja 2453

Preval 2349

Razor 2601

E shoulder

Kriški rob 2358

Vrh Zlebičev 2199

tarn 2154

62

81

81

88

N

NE

Kriški rob 2358

Trentska vrata 2387

Križ 2410

Stenarska vrata 2295

Stenar 2501

Dovški Phavec 2224

Sovatna Pass 2180

tarn 2154

88

83

84

84

A Y-shaped arrangement of ridges, open to the N above Gozd-
Martuljek. The group is relatively isolated and remote and
contains two well known mtns., Škrlatica - the second highest
summit of the E Julians, and Špik. These apart, there is little
of interest to walking/scrambling parties, whereas the entire
group is noted for its serious high quality rock climbing, in
recognition for which four bivouac huts, numbered I to IV,
serve all important approaches within the area.

DOVŠKI GAMSOVEC   2440m.
ROGLJICA   2465m.
DOLKOVA ŠPIČA   2582m.
RAKOVA ŠPIČA   2550m.

86. The first two and the last of these peaks rise on the escarpment running N from Kriška stena to Škrlatica. A large
spur projects SE behind Rogljica which at first gains height
across a saddle and culminates in Dolkova špiča before descending towards Vrata. Rogljica and Rakova špiča present
imposing NW faces of 600m. to the Krnica valley; several
rtes. of V/V+.

ŠKRLATICA   2738m.

Scarlet Crag. Formerly, Suhi Plaz. A craggy, distinctive
mtn. with a fairly frequented normal rte. and two prestigious
pillar climbs among others on the architecturally fine looking
but loose NW face; 600m., V. First ascent: J. Kugy with
A. Komac and A. Kravanja, 24 August, 1880.

South Side. The usual rte., a rough walk and scramble. Faded
waymarks, track poor in places, final section equipped with
rungs and cables. Gr. I.

87. From Bivouac IV (c. 2050m.) (2½ h. from Aljažev hut,
Rte. 22), return N along the approach to Vrata for a few min.
to the last junction. Waymark. Continue ahead N, past a L
turning to Kriška stena, over scrub and stones to the spur
descending SE from Dolkova špiča. The track crosses this by

a ledge system, narrow in places but short, then climbs the last vegetated slope to reach the upper cwm of Zadnji Dolek. A rough ascent across this stony hollow leads to the R side which is followed up to the W flank of the SE ridge of the mtn. Continue among large rocks to above a projection from the ridge, then scramble R and climb the ridge flank with cut steps and cables to the crest which leads to the summit ($2\frac{1}{2}$ h., 5 h. from Aljažev hut).

88. From Pogačnikov hut take the waymarked track N and pass junction on L for Razor. A broad terrace leads to a fork; keep L and cross a steep craggy slope with cables above the Križka tarn (2154m.) to reach further R a rock wall under the enclosing ridge of Kriški rob. An equipped path ascends this R-wards to the Trentska vrata (2387m.), merely a rubble shoulder W of Križ ($1\frac{1}{4}$ h.). This point is the true origin of the ridge running N to Škrlatica. Immediately N, the W side of the escarpment ridge forms a long rock wall called Kriška stena, above the Krnica valley; the lowest point in its crest, 2301m., is reached from that valley by a waymarked rte. with fixed cables, etc.

From the shoulder descend stony slopes by a small track to the Kriška stena exit, then descend R (NE) over rocky ground with a poor track to a fork (2143m.), waymark 'Škrlatica' (30 min.). Take the L branch, working NW and N over rocky terraces to cross the stony cwm (snow) under Dovški Gamsovec, and reach the red saddle of Rdeča škrbina between Rogljica and Dolkova špiča. (The latter can be attained in a few min.). Now descend N into the rock strewn upper cwm of Zadnji Dolek, normally with large snow banks, to join the previous rte. as it approaches the W side of the SE ridge ($1\frac{3}{4}$ h.). Continue by Rte. 87 to summit (45 min., $4\frac{1}{4}$ h. from Pogačnikov hut, $3\frac{3}{4}$ h. in reverse direction).

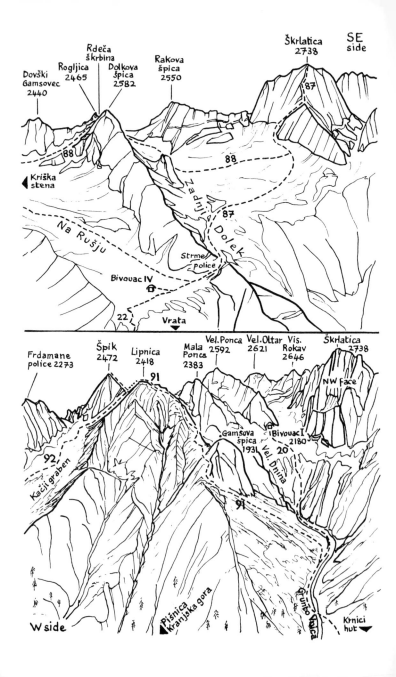

Dovški
Gamsovec
2440

Rogljica
2465

Rdeča
škrbina

Dolkova
špica
2582

Rakova
špica
2550

Škrlatica
2738

SE
side

87

88

Kriška
stena

88

Na Rušju

Zadnji Dolek

87

Strme
police

Bivouac IV

22

Vrata

Frdamane
police 2273

Špik
2472

Lipnica
2418

91

Mala
Ponca
2383

Vel. Ponca
2592

Vel. Oltar
2621

Viš.
Rokav
2646

Škrlatica
2738

NW face

92

Kačji graben

Gamsova
špica
1931

Bivouac I
2180

20

Vel. Dnina

91

W side

Pišnica
Kranjska gora

Krnica valley

Krnici
hut

VISOKI ROKAV   2646m.
VELIKI OLTAR   2621m.   (Mali, 2529m.)
ŠIROKA PEČ   2497m.

89. These summits follow Škrlatica to the N, where the ridge
bifurcates. The NE branch has no notable summit except, on
a spur to the N, Siroka peč, whose N face, with a profile and
configuration like the Grandes Jorasses, has half a dozen outstanding rock climbs of 700m., IV to VI, approached from
Bivouac III (2 h. by good path from Gozd-Martuljek).

VELIKA PONCA   2592m.
MALA PONCA   2383m.

90. The NW branch of the Y fork ridge commencing at Vel.
Oltar carries these two summits, easily reached by obvious
ridges from Bivouac I, before rising to Špik. Beyond Špik,
the Frdamane police (2273m.) has 600m. rtes. on its NE face
(Bivouac III).

ŠPIK   2472m.

Though not a mtn. of any great height, this peak rises with
triangular perfection from most viewpoints and is held in great
esteem by virtue of its tremendous N face, rising 950m. from
the Pod Screm screes above Gozd-Martuljek. First ascent,
probably by hunters in early 19th century. The lower forests
taken by the ordinary rtes. are breeding grounds for vipers.

From South-West. An interesting expedition with excellent
regional views along N side of range. The upper track is in
poor condition, waymarks faded. Gr. I.

91. From Krnici hut follow the level path E in woodland which
gradually ascends the R side of the Grunto Vnica. Below the
Grunt headland (1403m.) the path crosses the dry stream bed
to continue NE up the L side of the bed for some distance before turning away L in dwarf pine and scrub to reach scree
bands under Gamsova špiča. Keep below wall of latter and
cross its W ridge to vegetated slopes on the N side. The track

winds up these to the broad spur rising behind Gamsova špiča, which is followed up mainly by zigzags in scree and rocks on its L flank to the secondary top called Lipnica (2418m.). Descend shattered rocks N to a snow saddle and climb the easy summit ridge of Špik above (about $4\frac{1}{4}$ h.).

From West. A steep direct waymarked trail, in poor condition at present. Recommended as a quick descent to Kranjska gora. Gr. I.

92. Start at c. 900m. below the roadhead of Rtes. 8, 19, just before the bridge turning R with a lane returning to the Vršič road. A waymarked track on L ascends a forest opening and with increasing steepness near the stream continues under headland 1357m. where the stream goes underground. The ravine of Kačji graben cuts the entire W side of Špik above and cliffs enclose the dry stream bed. The track follows terraces on the L (N) side for a considerable distance and height, eventually traversing on to the upper broad scree/snow slopes of the ravine. Go up these to a snow couloir issuing from the gap between Špik and Lipnica, and so join Rte. 91 (about $5\frac{1}{4}$ h. from small road at bottom, $6 - 6\frac{1}{4}$ h. from Kranjska gora all the way on foot).

93. North Face. The original rte. by Anna Escher with Angelo Dibona, 11 October, 1925 avoids the challenge of the face by veering R at mid-height on to the NW facet, where a complicated way was pursued to the top (IV with pitch of V). The upper part of the face is now taken by at least three separate rtes., but the classic way and the easiest remains the first direct ascent to be made following the initiative given by the Dibona party: Mme. M. M. Pibernik (who led throughout) and Dr. S. Tominšek, 5-6 September, 1926 (950m., V with a pitch V+). One of the best limestone climbs of its class in the Alps. The rte. takes a line of chimneys and cracks R of centre

in the upper wall, and uses the Dibona approach in the lower
half, up a gully and grassy ramps/steps slanting R to a prominent grassy rockhead; from the top of this by rocks trending
L for 250m. to a vague ledge and line of steps rising R which
Dibona followed on to the NW facet. The direct ascent commences c. 50m. up this ledge system, and initially slants L to
reach the main chimney line in the upper face. 8 - 10 h. for
face. The Martuljek (Lipovčeva) inn (930m.) between Gozd-
Martuljek and Bivouac III is the best starting point ($2\frac{1}{2}$ h. to
foot of face - a rough complicated approach).

TRIGLAV AREA

CMIR   2393m.

94. A good viewpoint from a clifftop commanding Vrata. Gr. I-.
Waymarked trail from Staničeva hut along a grassy plateau/
corridor NW to saddle under Begunjski vrh, fork, from where
the path contours N side of latter summit to reach a long
slabby ridge running NE over the intermediate top of Rjavčeve
glave (2360m.) to Cmir (2 h.). There are noteworthy rock
climbs on NW face.

BEGUNJSKI VRH   2461m.

95. As for Cmir above, keeping L at fork on saddle; easily
combined with Cmir (1 h.).

VISOKA VRBANOVA ŠPIČA   2408m.

96. A 30 min. walk from Staničeva hut to the upper end of a
ridge which further N, in its more picturesque lower reaches,

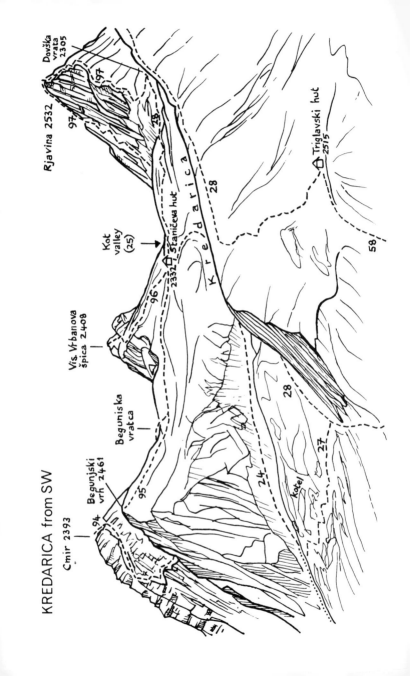

KREDARICA from SW

Cmir 2393

Begunjski vrh 2461

Begunjska vrata

Vis. Vrbanova špica 2408

Kot valley (25)

Staničewa hut 2332

Kredarica

Rjavina 2532

Dovška vrata 2305

Triglavski hut 2515

94

95

96

97

97

197

28

28

28

24

27

koča

58

encloses the upper part of the Kot valley.

RJAVINA   2532m.

Rust coloured mtn.   An attractive pyramid peak with twin
summits, ENE of Staničeva hut.   It has an imposing N face
above the Kot valley, 800m. high with good pillar climbs
(IV/V).

97. From the hut take waymarked trail towards Kredarica
and on a shoulder ignore fork R to latter.   Continue L to
another fork almost immediately.   Keep L again and descend
for 10 min. to reach the saddle of Dovška vrata (2305m.) below
WSW ridge of mtn.   Climb this fine steep narrow crest on its
R side with cables at two or three points to the first summit
then go along an airy crest to the highest point (2 h.), Gr. I.
The return route can be varied by descending a marked trail
down the NW facet; this starts midway between the two summits
and goes down steep rocks with cables in a descending traverse
at first, then more directly in zigzags to the Pekel hollow in
the upper Kot valley;   join the valley trail and go up directly
to the hut at the top ($1\frac{3}{4}$ h.), Gr. I+.

REŽ   2441m.

98. An elongated rock mass at the WNW end of the Kredarica
ridge.   It has an independent equipped trail to its summit,
branching R at the second fork before reaching the Dovška
vrata mentioned in Rte. 97.

VELIKI DRAŠKI VRH   2243m.

99. Has a relatively easy but unmarked route over grass and
scree on S side, reached from Rte. 29 (Rudno polje to Vodnikov

hut). The N face has big rock climbs.

MALI DRAŠKI VRH   2132m.

100. Similar to the parent summit above, to its E.

TOŠC   2275m.

101. Normal rte. unmarked but has small track from Vodnikov hut over the Bohinjska vratca (1979m.). Rock climbing on N/NW faces.

VERNAR   2225m.

102. A pendant to Tošc, the two divided by the track across the Bohinjska vratca, above Vodnikov hut.

KANJAVEC   2568m.

Ital: Monte degli Avvoltoi = Vultures' mtn. A large somewhat shapeless mtn. consisting of broken precipices 1500m. high on N side, overlooking Zadnjica (Trenta), and relatively tame slopes on the S. Much frequented by mtn. walkers, an excellent viewpoint. For the equipped traverse across N face, see Rte. 44 (II). First recorded ascent: J. Kugy, 18 August, 1877.

103. <u>South Side Routes.</u> Easy and popular, Gr. I-.

(I) Reach the Čez Hriberice saddle (2358m.) from Prehodavcih hut by Rte. 44 (I) in $1\frac{1}{2}$ h., or from the Tržaška hut by same rte. in reverse in 1 h. Waymarks, etc. at junction on saddle. Follow track over scree on L (S) side of spur coming down from mtn. and finish up a broad scree/snow gully to summit ridge. Follow ridge W to top (45 min. from saddle).

(II) The shortest way from Prehodavcih hut is to follow Rte. 44 (I) to the entrance of the Hriberice cwm at pt. 2274m.; junction of paths (1 h.). Take the L branch rising across the rocky cwm and continue directly to summit (1 h., 2 h. from hut).

104. <u>East Ridge.</u> From Tržaška hut, a more direct way than Rte. 103 (I). Gr. I. A small waymarked track runs SW under the E ridge, joining it rather more than halfway up. Follow the crest to a junction with Rte. 103 (I), hence the summit ($1\frac{1}{2}$ h. from hut). Note: This direct rte. has been much improved lately, and the track has new waymarks.

ŠPIČJE RIDGE   2398m.

105. A popular and recommended variation to Rte. 41 (Triglav Lakes hut to Prehodavcih hut). Gr. I, waymarked, cables and stanchions at various points. Follow Rte. 41 to below Kopica (on the enclosing ridge to E), about $1\frac{1}{2}$ km. before the Veliko (4th) lake (30 min.). A track forks L from the main one. Follow this to screes below Veliko Špičje (2398m.) and ascend a rough narrow cwm on its R side to ridge pt. 2355m. Spectacular view (2 h.). (By leaving path and following ridge SW, Vel. Špičje can be reached in 20 min.). Continue along the fine rocky ridge NE over pt. 2320m. to Malo Špičje (2312m.) and Zad. Lopa (2115m.), from where a short descent leads to the Prehodavcih hut (1 h., $3\frac{1}{2}$ h. from Triglav Lakes hut).

VELIKA TIČARICA   2091m.
MALA TIČARICA   2071m.

Adjoining bold rockfaces overlooking the Triglav Lakes hut, a short and popular excursion. Gr. I-.

106. From the Triglav Lakes hut return S along the approach path for a few min. to a L fork (signpost). Ascend open woodland in zigzags to grass and scree running up into a gully with fixed ropes giving access to the Štapce col (1851m.). On the other side fork L (N) up a slope on the R side of the main ridge to a shoulder. Here a L fork rises in a few min. to the Mala summit (1 h.). Return and continue by the main track N below R side of ridge, quite rough on scree and blocks, to another L fork rising to the Velika top (20 min.).

JALOVEC AREA

TRAVNIK 2379m.

107. Flat grassy place (refers to an isolated spot on mtn., otherwise totally out of character). The principal intermediate summit on the long and fairly level ridge running SW from Mojstrovka to Jalovec, originating near the Vršič pass and dividing at a tangent the Trenta and Planica valleys. The S slopes above Trenta are crowned by characteristic 'roof' slabs which are a feature along all this side of the ridge. There is no waymarked or normal rte., and the summit is rarely visited by walkers. The S side has a small, vague and complicated track which serves as a descent rte. from climbs undertaken on the NW face. It works NE below ridge crest and soon descends a gully to reach a long traverse track running NE to the Grebenec saddle (1983m.) below Mojstrovka on Rte. 72. Alternatively, the main ridge crest can be traversed to Mojstrovka (Gr. II).

The NW face above the Planica valley is one of the largest rock walls in the Julian Alps and forms part of a cliff extending nearly 5 km. from Mojstrovka to Jalovec. It reaches a height of 900m. and is regarded as an outstanding rock climbing zone, easily approached from Planinski/Tamar hut in 2 h. or so. The classic rte. is the Aschenbrenner (1934), which starts from a hollow at the top of a wooded rocky ravine in the summit line. A central dièdre/depression is reached by a long traverse in from the R. The R side of the depression is climbed until a great ramp slanting L halfway up the face can be joined and followed to exposed upper walls which are taken direct to the top (12 h., 800m., VI). There are rtes. of similar difficulty to the L and R of the Aschenbrenner. At the far

R (W) side of the face a large spur divides this wall section from that of Šite. It gives a good rte. of 700m., mainly III with pitches of IV. It is the easiest rte. anywhere up the 5 km. wall.

ŠITE   2234m.   2310m.   2307m.

108. The continuation ridge and wall SW of Travnik, with similar characteristics to latter and comparable access problems. The summit ridge is sharp and exposed. The easiest descent rte. goes down the S side over a rock barrier and steep grass/rubble slopes for nearly 400m. until a traverse SW can be made into the hollow below Jalovška škrbina (q.v.), whence the Planica valley or Trenta can be reached by way-marked rtes.

The NW face is part of the same wall below Travnik, but now rises some 550m. from the Mali Kot screes at the top of the Planica valley. Half a dozen rtes. climb the broad wall, with pitches of VI+ and A3. The Great Dièdre (1954) at the R side is one of the hardest free climbs in the Julian Alps. To its L is the Šite Pillar (1966), a harder and partially artificial rte. There are several rtes. of V+ or harder further L.

JALOVŠKA ŠKRBINA   2110m.

Between Šite and Goličica (Jalovec), an important, deep ridge gap providing the best ascent/descent rte. to and from the Šite ridge and offering a descent/ascent alternative to and from Jalovec, to avoid the Jalovec couloir.

109. NE (Planica) side. Gr. II. Waymarks faded, fixed cables and pegs missing or loose. From the Planinski/Tamar hut follow the main valley trail which is quite good up to the stony Mali Kot (c. 1600m.), the upper valley directly below the impressive Jalovec profile. A poor and steeper track continues up scree and rubble to the broad opening of the long Jalovec couloir, on the L side of the lowest rock toe of Jalovec ($2\frac{1}{2}$ h.). Slant L on steep scree or snow, and just under a big rock island at the L side of the couloir move L to enter a parallel secondary gully; climb this, normally with steep snow patches, and

old cables on L side to a terrace at the top. Go up a little then make a steep rising traverse L in rocks with cables and pegs for 60m. to a near vertical wall below the col. Go straight up in an exposed position with loose and dangling ironmongery but good ledges/stances to an abrupt finish in 20m. In descent an experienced party should not need to abseil (1 h., $3\frac{1}{2}$ h. from Planinski hut; $2\frac{1}{4}$ h. in descent).

110. SW (Trenta) side. Gr. I-. Waymarks faded but small track quite good to within 20 min. of pass. From Vršič follow Rte. 17 to the three-way fork just after the closed chalet ($1\frac{1}{2}$ h.). Take the small R-hand branch marked Jalovška škrbina/ Jezerca, steeply through trees; due to undergrowth pay attention to the meanderings of the track. Reach a steep grassy zone and go up this in the same general WNW direction to broad scree and rubble. So emerge at the entrance to a boulder hollow; in the middle of this is a large rock with rte. indications painted on it (c. 2000m.). Cross the hollow in the same direction, track and waymarks virtually gone, and rise gradually to the col at the back (2 h., $3\frac{1}{2}$ h. from Vršič; $2\frac{1}{2}$ h. in descent).

JALOVEC 2643m.

Ger: Jalouc. Ital: Jalouz, Jalluz, Gialluz, etc. = Dry or Barren mtn. Easily the finest and most picturesque summit in the Yugoslav Julians. The much admired profile from the Planica valley (NE) side forms the insignia adopted by the PZS (Slovene Alpine Association) for its badge, etc. "PZS" is painted in letters 2m. high on the summit. Jalovec is essentially a mountaineers' peak, serious by any approach except in very good conditions. Its specialised rock climbs involve longish approaches coupled with general mountaineering technique throughout. The summit area is marked by a great sloping slabby roof tilted to the N in two or three tiers, up which most of the major climbs finish. The rock is generally good throughout but care is needed to avoid dislodging loose material on easy-angled rock.

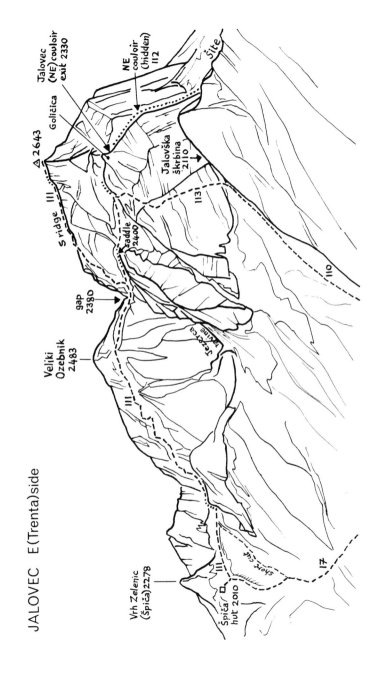

JALOVEC E(Trenta) side

△ 2643

S. ridge III

Golička

Jalovec (NE) couloir exit 2330

NE couloir (hidden) 112

Šite

Jalovška škrbina 2110

113

110

Saddle 2400

gap 2380

Veliki Ozebnik 2483

III

Tešenica ravine

III

Vrh Zelenic (Špica) 2278

III

Špica hut 2010

short cut

17

First ascent: C. Wurmb with M. Černuta and A. Štrugulc, 2 August, 1875. In winter: G. Bolaffio, A. Krammer, J. Kugy with J. Komac and A. Oitzinger, 27 December, 1900.

South Ridge. The easiest rte. and a common finish for at least three other approaches, of which the shortest and simplest by far is that from the Špiča hut. A fine little climb with numerous cables, rungs and cut holds in ground otherwise giving moves of II+. Gr. I+. Main rte. 1 waymarks generously displayed throughout. Ice axe advisable. First ascent: K. Blodig, solo, 16 September, 1878 (by a dangerous variant).

111. From the Špiča hut descend the approach path for 5 min., to 100m. distance beyond the base of the grassy buttress on which the hut stands; a track forks L from the Trenta valley trail. (Don't try to traverse from a higher point near the hut). Follow the branch track horizontally N to rubble and boulders then a snowfield which is crossed fairly high up but only in a slightly rising traverse to rocks below an obvious saddle in the SE ridge of Veliki Ozebnik. Take steep rocks in a shallow gully and just below saddle veer L and climb several good pitches to reach the SE ridge. Leave the ridge immediately and commence a series of rising traverses R (N) alternating with upward pitches, across the E face of Vel. Ozebnik; some unexpected movements L. Eventually pass well below summit of this secondary mtn. where the traverse R levels out and rounds a couple of small shoulders to reach scree and a snow-field. Descend snow somewhat L (NNW), passing close to the cavernous exit from the couloir/gap (2380m.) dividing Vel. Ozebnik and Jalovec proper. From a little snow saddle (directly above the Jezerca ravine used by Blodig) ascend half L on steepish snow to join rocks below S ridge in a few min. (1$\frac{1}{2}$ h.). Short chimneys and generally slabby rock trending L then R lead to the S ridge crest above its gable end. Follow the crest precisely, quite exposed at one point, to a notch

below the summit step. Move L and climb a series of loose ledges and short gullies to rejoin the ridge about 50m. level walking from the summit (45 min. , $2\frac{1}{4}$ h. from Špiča hut, $1\frac{1}{2}$ h. in descent).

Jalovec Couloir (NE Ordinary Route). Probably the most classic rte. of its class in the Yugoslav Julians, for climbers only. The couloir (Jalovčev ozebnik) makes a deep incision between the walls of Jalovec and Goličica, at the top of the Planica valley, and is conspicuous in all views from therein. The snowbed has an average angle of 45°, nearly 50° in places, is 300m. high and in the narrower upper half is normally exposed to stonefall after 11.00 am. Not recommended for descent. Ice axe essential, crampons useful. Technically only Gr. I+ in good hard snow conditions. Faded waymarks, no aids in couloir. First ascent: J. Kugy with A. Komac, 7 September, 1884.

112. From the Planinski/Tamar hut (1108m.) follow Rte. 109 to the base of the couloir ($2\frac{1}{2}$ h.). On steepening snow climb keeping close to the R wall, the gully narrowing all the while towards the top; exit on a snow/scree saddle (c. 2330m.) with waymarks on boulders ($1\frac{1}{4}$ h.). Keep R, close to the rockface of Jalovec (stonefall possible) and traverse snow and rocks SW to another saddle, slightly higher, about 200m. distance away. Cross this in the same direction and traverse a steepish snow slope, not far, to join Rte. 111 where it starts up rocks below the gable end of the S ridge (30 min.). Continue by Rte. 111 to the summit (45 min. , 5 h. from Planinski hut).

By the Škrbina/Goličica trails. Frequented by parties coming from the Planinski/Tamar hut, after climbing the Jalovec couloir (Rte. 112), as the safest descent rte. Sometimes followed by enterprising parties coming from Vršič direct, spurning an overnight halt at the Špiča hut, but in any event

109

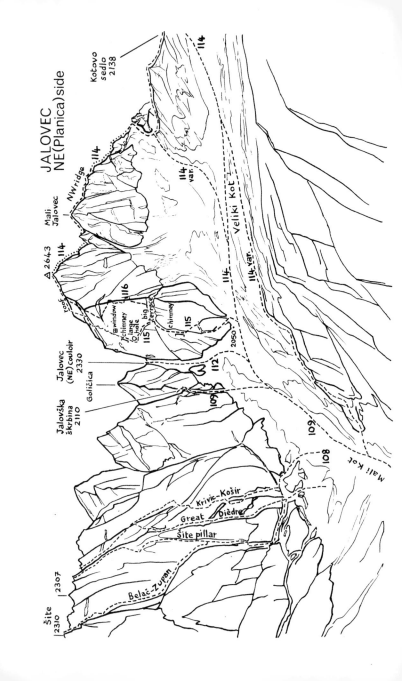

JALOVEC
NE (Planica) side

Kotovo sedlo 2138

NW ridge

Mali Jalovec

114

114 var.

Veliki Kot

114 var.

△ 2643

114

116

roof

window

chimney

large O hole

115

big terrace

chimney

115

115

2050

Jalovec (NE) couloir 2330

Goličica

112

109

Jalovška škrbina 2110

109

108

Mali Kot

Šite 2307

Krivic-Košir

Great Diedre

Šite pillar

Belač-Župan

Šite 2310

wanting a more interesting scramble than the ordinary rte. Recommended to experienced mtn. scramblers. Gr. II. Originally well equipped with cables, etc., now in a bad state of repair, waymarks, etc. faded.

113. From the Planinski/Tamar hut follow Rte. 109 to Jalovška škrbina (2110m.) and descend into the boulder hollow on SE side for a few min. to reach a large boulder with painted waymarkings at c. 2000m. $(3\frac{3}{4}$ h.).

From Vršič follow Rte. 100 to the large marker boulder $(3\frac{1}{4}$ h.).

From the marker boulder traverse horizontally SW for a few min. to the foot of the E facet of Goličica. An equipped trail goes up this 200m. wall, first by a ramp to L then in continuous little chimneys and steps with several free moves of II. At the top emerge on a slight shoulder and follow easy waymarked rocks under S face of Goličica to reach broken ground adjoining the exit saddle above the Jalovec couloir $(1\frac{1}{4}$ h.). Continue by Rtes. 112, 111 to summit $(1\frac{1}{4}$ h., $6\frac{3}{4}$ h. from Planinski hut, $5\frac{3}{4}$ h. from Vršič pass. In descent from summit: to Planinski hut, 4 h.; to Vršič, $3\frac{1}{2}$ h. The easiest descent to Vršič is via the Špiča hut, Rte. 111).

North-West Ridge (from Kotovo sedlo). One of the finest mountaineering rtes. of its class in the Yugoslav Julians. Originally equipped with cables, etc. as a descent rte., now in a bad state of repair; waymarks almost indiscernible; route finding demands experience. Due (unfortunately) to be re-equipped in 1978/79 because of great 'demand' - when the standard will presumably fall to Gr. I+. At present, several pitches of II/II+. Excellent situations, exposed. Highly recommended. First ascent: T. Maischberger, H. Pfannl, A. von Radio-Radiis, V. Wessely, 4 June, 1900.

114. From the Planinski/Tamar hut follow Rte. 109 to scree

and snow below the Jalovec couloir ($2\frac{1}{2}$ h.). Turn sharp R and ascend steep rubble, tedious, or snow, due N in a shallow depression which leads to the level Veliki Kot hollow under the NW ridge. Higher up bear L over very stony ground, with grass re-appearing, to reach the conspicuous saddle of Kotovo sedlo (2138m.) (1 h. , $3\frac{1}{2}$ h. from hut).

Alternatively, a short-cut and better rte. is to leave the Mali Kot path where it becomes poor at c. 1600m. in the main valley bed, directly under the Šite wall. Here a small track (waymark) branches R (W) and winds up a very steep grass spur to rockbands and ledges under the escarpment edge supporting the Vel. Kot hollow. At the top of the spur the track, now poor, trends L in dwarf pine and rocks to reach the escarpment, after which it peters out in stones where the first approach is joined about 20 min. from the saddle (3 h. from hut). In descent the start of the track is very difficult to locate.

A short-cut for both approaches, when halfway up the stony Vel. Kot hollow, is to veer L (WSW) to avoid Kotovo sedlo and join the foot of the NW ridge proper beyond an initial ridge hump; turn its lower rocks on steep scree/snow well to L before returning R to reach the ridge beyond the hump (saves 15 min.).

From Kotovo sedlo follow the ridge crest over a grassy hump to a short level section, rising again to below a rocky shoulder. Turn this on the R side, climbing broken slabs which bend round to rejoin the crest higher up. Follow the sharp crest on its R side by fine exposed slabs (II) to the top of Mali Jalovec. Now descend across a sensational double gap divided by a pinnacle which gives pitches of II+ in ascent and descent to its far side; its immediate top is turned on the R side. From the second gap work R, descending briefly to a ledge system which rises gradually below the steep terminal step of the NW ridge, to reach narrow terraces under the S ridge. Finish L up an open boulder gully to reach the S ridge crest in a little gap at the foot of its summit step where Rte. 111 is joined a few min. from the top ($2\frac{1}{2}$-3 h., 6-$6\frac{1}{2}$ h. from Planinski hut).

North-East Wall (Horn Route). The original and easiest rte. on the front face of the prominent jutting bastion of the mtn. which supports its characteristic 'roof'. One of the finest rtes. of its class in the Julian Alps and in the Eastern Alps as a whole. Varied pitches on mainly good rock. 400m., III with 3 pitches of IV-/IV. First ascent: Ferdinand Horn, solo, 1 August, 1909.

115. From the Planinski/Tamar hut follow Rte. 109 to below the Jalovec couloir. Slant R to lowest rock toe of the wall and start 30m. up to R from this point ($2\frac{1}{2}$ h.).

Climb diagonally L up a series of small gullies with loose rock for 50m. to a terrace below steep slabs which are cut up to the L by a fine chimney/couloir. Move R along the narrowing terrace cutting through the slab zone for 20m. and finish up a short gully (III) to a thin ledge below an overhang. Follow ledge L into a chimney pitch of the chimney/couloir mentioned above, and climb this (IV-) to a continuation gully then broken rock steps trending R to the L end of a large scree terrace about one third way up the wall on its R side. Within a few m. of reaching the terrace (do not go higher up it), continue straight up the wall above (L), in a short gully and exit L to the first of numerous inconsistent ledges rising in a steep line to L. The correct and best rte. across and up pitches linking these ledges for c. 100m. is not easy to find. After two distinct short steps between the first three ledges a longer pitch trends L up a vague continuation line above a very steep wall to a ledge/stance. Here a narrow ramp slanting L again is taken; before reaching its top step L (cairn) along a ledge which leads to a large cave. Climb the outer L edge of the cave direct (III) then move L into a fine chimney rising for 50m. Climb this in two pitches of IV (some old pegs in place), turning an upper overhang on its R side. Exit L along a little overhung terrace, from the upper end of which ascend trending R to the top of a large window/hole formed at the head of the main wall (3 h.). Now scramble a succession of slabs and low rock steps (II) forming the lower part of the roof, up to a significantly bigger step which divides the roof into two main parts. A broken groove (20m., II), L of a vague gully slanting R, cuts this about centre. The upper narrower roof is easy and sometimes snow covered, reaching to the summit without incident (1 h. , 4 h. from foot of wall, $6\frac{1}{2}$ h. from hut).

116.   North-East Pillar (Comici Route).   Among numerous rtes. on the NE and N flanks of the Jalovec bastion, the dividing pillar edge is the most striking feature of the area. Probably the most classic and frequently climbed rte. of its standard in the Julian Alps, on excellent rock. Although the original rte. was made in 1932, a party led by E. Comici straightened it out in 1934 to produce a climb of IV and V, sustained, with 2 pitches of V+ and one of A1, with 20 pegs normally in place. Approach as for Horn rte. to the large terrace one third way up the face, from where, to R, the pillar edge is climbed mainly on its L side. Sustained section therefrom, 180m. Time from base to summit, 8 h.

VELIKI OZEBNIK   2483m.

117.   Immediately S of Jalovec; its E flank is traversed high up by Rte. 111.   From end of this traverse, at the highest snowfield, the summit can be reached in 15 min. by Gr. I rocks (E side of its N ridge). Otherwise of no interest.

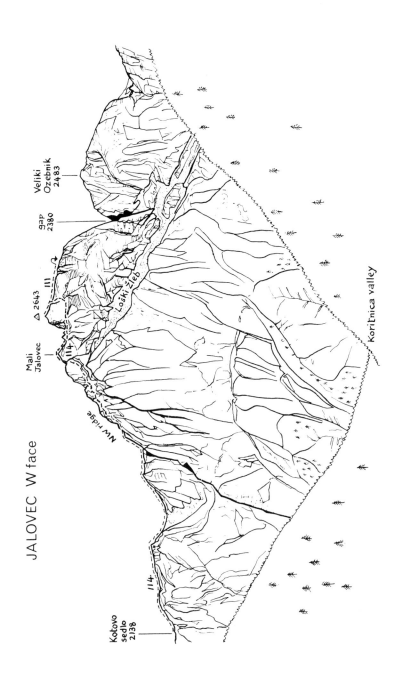

JALOVEC W face

Veliki Ozebnik 2483

gap 2380

△ 2643

111

Loški Žleb

Mali Jalovec

114

NW ridge

114

Kotovo sedlo 2138

Koritnica valley

PELC NAD KLONICAMI   2437m.

118.   A fine little rock peak overlooking the Škrbina za Gradom pass, SW of Špiča hut. The first of several interesting rock points running S to Skutnik (2172m.), eventually Bavški Grintavec. First ascent: J. Kugy and A. Komac, 1891. Good short climbs on sound rock. A waymarked track traverses S and SW from Špiča hut to the Škrbina (2250m.), 45 min. The short steep NW ridge above the pass gives a popular climb along a sharp exposed crest, commenced from L side up a gully, with short pitches of III (1½ h.). The obvious E ridge flanking approach to pass is mostly III with a crux pitch of V. The complete traverse S to Nizki vrh (2114m.), and from there small descent track to Trenta, supplies the best rock scramble (III) to be made from Špiča hut.

BAVŠKI GRINTAVEC   2344m.

Crumbling Mtn. of Bovec. A prominent topographical summit situated at the head of Zad. Trenta valley in a fairly remote and isolated position but approached by good tracks from three directions, spasmodically waymarked and partly equipped. Extensive panorama. First ascent: I. Mlekuž and E. Trancer, 1868.

<u>From Zad. Trenta by North Ridge</u>. Virtually all ascents are made by this rte. An excellent training walk, quite worthwhile. Gr. I.

119.   From the Soča source inn (Rte. 2) follow the unmade lane in valley bed which after 30 min. continues past chalets as a path for some distance to a short zigzag section in open forest, followed by a gradual ascent to a fork. Keep R and ascend to Zapotek alp (1385m.) (2 h.). The easy path now leads to a steep ascent under the NE side of the mtn., to a triple junction. Ascend R (W) in zigzags over grass, rocks and snow patches to a large saddle, Kanja (2030m.) at foot of N ridge (1½ h.).

A little track goes up grooves on R side of an initial ridge step (cables) to a sloping scree/snow shoulder, followed by a fine terminal rock ridge with aids in places (1 h., $4\frac{1}{2}$ h. from inn).

Note: There is a more direct rte. across the large, conspicuous snow/scree terrace slanting up R to the sloping shoulder on N ridge. This terrace cuts the NE face almost in two parts and is reached by a rough track over two rockbands cut by gullies, from the triple fork. Gr. II-, much loose rock. The NE ridge, approached by a small track to the Vel. vrata pass (1841m.), is a good rock rte., Gr. II.

PONCA GROUP

120. The Italo-Yugoslav frontier ridge enclosing W side of the Planica valley carries several peaks of some interest, most of which have equipped trails in a poor state of repair. From N to S: Vis. Ponca (2274m.), Srednja Ponca (2228m.), Zad. Ponca (2242m.), Strmi Strug (2265m.), Vevnica, or Veunza (2340m.), V. Koncu špiča, or Monte Termine (2350m.), Kotova špiča (2376m.), preceeding Kotovo sedlo (3128m.) (Rte. 114). Vevnica (J. Kugy with A. and J. Komac, 1898) is an outstanding rock peak approached from the Italian side by an impressive and not altogether easy equipped trail called the Via della Vita. The NE ridge also has an old and quite complicated equipped trail. On the N side there are first class rock climbs of up to 800m., generally Gr. V or harder.

MANGRT AREA

MANGRT 2677m.

Ital: Monte Mangart. Ger: Manhart = Mango-like mtn. One of the outstanding viewpoints of the Julian Alps, an isolated summit dome when viewed from the E and S, but seen from the N (Ital.) side rather lost at the end of an immense rock wall closing the Fusine Lakes valley. The Ital. side is much less accessible for parties visiting the main areas of the Yugo. Julians and its ordinary rtes. are quite long. Conversely, the Yugo. (S and W) side is much frequented owing to road access to the Mangrtu hut at nearly 2000m. First recorded ascent: F. von Hohenwart, 20 August, 1794. In winter: A. Gstirner with J. Pinter, 12 February, 1893.

North Side Terrace. The easiest rte., circuitous, which traverses a belt of slabs and a continuation snow terrace across the top of N face on Ital. side of mtn. below the summit dome, and returns up the rounded terminal part of the E ridge. The snow terrace is exposed and requires care when a trail across it is absent, or in icy conditions. Gr. I on account of this, ice axe necessary.

121. From the Mangrtu hut cross pasture NE on a small track which contours not far above the 'ring road' round the hut; then cross road and continue on grass to the frontier ridge where a good path follows below the crest. It passes under and S of the grassy shoulder called Strmi Nos (2197m.) of Mte. Traunig (2204m.) and continues E to pass just below the Forcella Mangart (2166m.), then under the S side of Rateški Mali Mangrt (2259m., called by the Italians, Piccolo Mangart, 2263m.). After this the frontier ridge is joined and followed in a few min. to a little saddle directly under the rock walls running R to form the W facet of the mtn. The path bears L (E) over saddle and soon forks, waymarks (30 min.). Keep L over stones, blocks and snowpatches where the track is vague, and follow up below steep rocks on R to a zone of smooth low-angled slabs. Ascend these along an obvious line to where they level out above the N face. Now a terrace stretches almost horizontally in the same direction, the latter part of it on snow shelving outwards at 20°. At the far end climb trending R to a better path on the broad E ridge. Go up quite steeply at first

on grass and rocks on L side of ridge to the top $(1\frac{1}{4}$ h., $1\frac{3}{4}$ h. from hut).

West Face Gully. Much the best and most direct way for experienced rock scramblers. A number of steep and exposed pitches with large iron spikes in the main gully of 250m. or on its R-hand retaining rib. Gr. I+.

122. From the Mangrtu hut follow Rte. 121 to fork in the path, just below L side of the W facet of the mtn. Take the R branch and follow it over rough ground in a few min. to the foot of a big obvious gully dividing the L side of the W facet and a large rock pillar further L (45 min.). To the L climb a steep ramp forming a subsidiary entrance, which leads up R to a small shoulder from where a short descent gives access to the gully bed. Climb the bed for 40m. then trend R up the side of a steep step to the rib at its top. Continue up steps on the rib to re-enter the bed near top of gully (snow), and so reach broken rock round a little hollow adjoining a shoulder immediately R. Now climb diagonally L for 30m. below a rock step above the shoulder, and reach the top of this step by a little gully R in 20m. Trend R over rough ground to a broad spur orientated SW, which soon leads to summit $(1\frac{1}{4}$ h., 2 h. from hut).

123. Italian North Side Route. An equipped rock climb only 20 years old has been specially constructed, merely to make the ascent on this side more interesting. However, this side of the mtn. is rarely adopted by mtn. scramblers, while the original rte. further R, taking a small track up to the Forcella Mangart to join Rte. 121, remains easier and quicker. The equipped rte. has numerous vertical and exposed pitches of Gr. II for 400m. It starts a short distance above the Nogara biv. hut (1850m., $2\frac{1}{2}$ h. by waymarked path from Upper Fusine Lakes inn). It reaches the slabs crossed by Rte. 121, and from

the upper end of these continues in a direct line towards the summit (3 h. from biv. hut).

124. <u>East Ridge.</u>   An impressive barrier crest marking the Yugo.-Italian frontier.   The N side displays the extensive N face of the Mangrt group which only relents towards its E end at the Sagherza pass (2149m.).   Above and E of this col the ridge rises steeply into the complex group of V. Konču špiča, Vevnica and Kotova špiča (see Rte. note 120).   The S side, along to the Sagherza pass, is mostly an unclimbed, gully-seamed, grassy rockface.   The ridge is normally reached at the Sagherza pass, but the approaches do not arrive at the pass itself exactly.   From the Ital. (N) side by an old equipped and waymarked rte. constituting part of the military Via della Vita, for climbers only, Gr. II (3 h. from Zacchi hut above Fusine Lakes).   From the Yugo. (S) side by a long but good waymarked path out of Gor. Log hamlet (650m.) up the Koritnica valley, Gr. I- with a short headwall turned on L, of Gr. I ($4\frac{1}{4}$ h.). From the pass the ridge itself is long and interesting, mainly over steep ground on its L (S) side, sometimes on the crest, with traces of a path and the remains of old cables and stanchions in places, Gr. II.   After a short ascent near the crest, a considerable descending traverse of c. 150m. is made under the crest on S side, below Piccolo Mangart di Coritenza (Koritniški Mali Mangrt, 2393m. or 2333m.); the ridge is rejoined further along at a small rock gap called Mala Forca (Huda Škrbina, 2401m. or 2362m.).   Thereafter narrow ledges are taken just below crest to join Rte. 121 near the summit (3 h. from Sagherza col).   First descended (and continued to Kotova špiča) by T. Keidel and H. Pfannl, 6 June, 1897.

125. <u>North Face Routes.</u>   A number of very serious climbs have been made on the extensive rock wall enclosing the head of the Fusine Lakes valley.   On the section forming the multi-

pillared N face of Piccolo Mangart di Coritenza the wall attains 800m. with rtes. of V+ or harder.

RATEŠKI MALI MANGRT 2259m. (Piccolo Mangart, 2263m.)

126. A secondary rock peak on the frontier ridge (Rte. 121), rising immediately above the Mangrtu hut, 20 min. walking distance away. It has excellent short climbs on sound rock, by its ridges Gr. II with short bits of III, or by a variety of climbs on S face (150m.) up to Gr. V, some of which are scratched and obvious. Recommended.

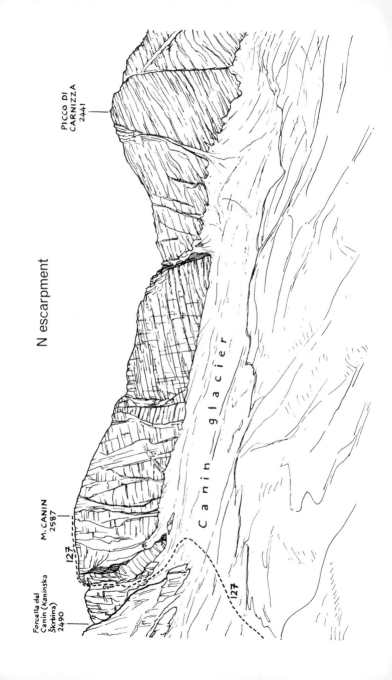

N escarpment

PICCO DI CARNIZZA 2441

M. CANIN 2587

Forcella del Canin (Kaninska Škrbina) 2490

127

Canin glacier

127

West Julian summits

MONTE CANIN   2587m.

Slov: Visoki Kanin = rocky pile. An important frontier summit at the junction of three ridges. Most of the history of Canin concerns the N (Ital.) side of the mtn. Even in recent times, before the Slov. Petra Skalarja hut (1811m.) above Bovec was destroyed, ascents on the S (Yugo.) side were relatively few. An old waymarked trail on this side, well shown on PZS map, is still in fairly good condition and can be followed without difficulty at Gr. I- (6-7 h., or 4 h. from Prestreljenikom cableway).
    A characteristic stratified limestone nappe escarpment marks all the N side, extending for $2\frac{1}{2}$ km. mostly with a wall height of 150m. (max. 250m.) above the terrace-type Canin gl., which is quite steep in places under the wall. This is the largest glacier as such in the Julian Alps. The rock is generally loose; numerous climbs have been made along the escarpment but none is recommended. Normal rtes. breach this wall in couloir/depressions and along lateral ledges. Canin has a S summit (2571m.), rarely visited. The N escarpment projects W as a ridge into Italy and soon dies down after Picco di Carnizza (2441m.). The main part of it marks the frontier ridge running E towards Prevala (col, 2067m.), close to which one fairly independent summit can be distinguished from several secondary tops along the ridge: Monte Forato (Prestreljenik, 2498m.).
    First ascent: probably about 1750. Recorded ascent by O. Sendtner in 1841. In winter: G. Bolaffio and J. Kugy with A. Oitzinger and G. Filafer, 12 January, 1902.

North Side normal route (Via Julia). A rib and secondary gully situated on the R side of the first large gully depression L of summit. Stonefall danger, fixed cables and iron rungs, ice axe advisable. Accurately marked up to the rock wall on all IGM and PZS maps. Gr. I.

127. From the Gilberti hut a good waymarked path rises gently up a little grassy valley W to a saddle (2005m.) under Bila peč, and continues in an easy contouring movement to cross the

first stream outlet from the gl. above. After rounding a little spur reach a waymarked fork (30 min.) at pt. 2018m. Leave the traverse path and take a small track L (SW) up the rubble slopes towards the gl., with several snowbeds. Above a little tarn which is passed on its L side the track is vague; continue in the same direction at a moderate angle between outcrops to a snow tongue leading on to the Canin gl. Ascend this trending slightly R, crevasses nearly in same direction, to below a large gully/depression L of the summit N wall. Go into the entrance between a narrow rock spur on R and a wall extending L ($1\frac{1}{4}$ h.). Climb a short, fairly steep snow slope near spur on R and get on to the rocks at a large painted indicator. Go up two steep pitches with ample metal rungs to a broken crest above any stonefall danger. Trend R into a steep subsidiary gully of mixed rock and snow and climb this direct with almost continuous cables to the main ridge above. Follow the ridge up a short step on large scratched holds to an easy walkway running along the now almost level crest to summit cairn (1 h., $2\frac{3}{4}$ h. from hut).

Note: At the entrance to the main couloir/depression the rock wall on L side has a series of stepped ledges running L across it, away from the summit direction, with access to the first ledge marked by a large painted indicator. This is the original 'Ledges Route', more exposed and at Gr. II somewhat more technical than the Via Julia. It reaches the frontier ridge after a considerable rising movement L, waymarks and old ironmongery, then returns along crest or on its L (S) side, over the Forc. del Canin, to reach the top. This is the rte. marked on maps and is climbed fairly often (3 h. from hut).

MONTE FORATO   2498m.

128. Slov: Prestreljenik = Holed mtn., an opening that pierces the SW ridge under its lowest point at c. 2350m. An excellent

viewpoint immediately above the upper sta. of the Prestrel-jenikom cableway (2200m.), and therefore frequented on the Yugoslav side, by waymarked path to col (2282m.) above sta., then by a short descent to a L fork (R for Prevala, Rte. 51) which leads up grassy rocks then over rubble and rocky terraces to R on to the NE ridge which is followed to summit (50 min.). Similarly by the track over Prevala (2067m.) from the Ital. side in 1¼ h. from latter col. On the Ital. side a direct rte. can be taken up to the hole, and from above it an exposed ledge traverse L to join the SW ridge, interesting, old waymarks, loose rock demands experience, Gr. II. First recorded ascent: O. Sendtner, 1841.

PREVALA   2067m.

An important pedestrian crossing on the frontier at the E end of the Canin group, see Rtes. 50, 51.

The following descriptions and notes refer to summits situated entirely in Italy and to the N of the Nevea saddle pass (1190m.).

MONTE CIMONE   2379m.

Slov: Strma peč = steep rock. The furthest W of the major summits of the W Julians. An imposing fortress-like mtn. of some complexity; great rock walls on all sides except the SE although the numerous technical rtes. are seldom done. The best known of these is the W face Comici (1930, 500m., V+). Steep vegetated approaches are a hindrance; the rock is generally sound but smooth and unfavourable for pegging. First ascent: H. Findenegg, 1878. In winter: M. Cesca and G. Stauderi, 25 January, 1932.

South-East Side (Viene Route).   The only easy way up and down the mtn. The rte. passes through breeding grounds for vipers - be warned. Gr. I.

129. The approach uses the well marked Via Alta traverse path which runs W from the Altipiano del Montasio, high above the Raccolana valley and below the S side of the M. Cimone group. At the start (Montasio end) this path is incorrectly

shown on all maps, inasmuch as it is indicated as originating at pt. 1576m., due N of the Pecol chalets (1519m.), the former pt. being a vague junction on the main approach to the Jôf di Montasio. A discontinuous minor track runs W from near the Brazzà hut to pt. 1576. If coming from this hut do not attempt to use this minor track; instead descend the approach Rte. 54 and return down the lane to the Pecol chalets. (The track which can be picked up near pt. 1576 runs W and parallel above the Via Alta and does not connect with it - it peters out).

The correct access to the traverse path uses a forest road running W from the end of the motorable road at the Pecol chalets (this is a wing of the motorable road going up to a chalet marked 1519m. and continuing E to the Parte di Mezzo chalets, 1552m.). At the Pecol chalets follow the forest road in a descending movement round to N and reach a big bend where it turns SW in 5 min. Just round this bend the Via Alta path forks R (W) and traverses pleasant forest; about one km. distance along the path is the point where the track on map is joined, not evident on the ground. Continue across steeper forest slopes, cross a little gorge and pass round a small spur to reach open pasture in a side valley drained by the Livinal di Vandul (stream, probably dry). The path continues W, more or less horizontally round grassy spurs and past a chalet (1573m.) to turn the base of the Pizzo Viene and traverse into the well defined bed of a narrow valley below the Viene cwm ($1\frac{1}{2}$ h.).

Leave the Via Alta trail and climb grass slopes N on the R side of the stream bed, getting steeper and rougher up to the cwm entrance and occasionally with traces of a discontinuous track. Ascend the cwm at a slightly easier angle due N towards the Forca della Viene (2083m.) at the top. About 75m. below this low relief saddle bear L (W) up steep grass slopes in the summit direction, merging into stones and rubble. Keep below a series of rock ribs jutting down from the E ridge above and to the R, and near the top, on steep loose blocks trend L round a low rock barrier and return R to the summit (2 h., $3\frac{1}{2}$ h. from roadhead at Pecol chalets).

JÔF DI MONTASIO   2753m.

Slov: Poliški Špik.   Ger: Montasch = Mountain summit (as 'of the region/range').   A magnificent mtn. with extensive rock walls cut by deep ravines.   Essentially a mtn. of cliffs with no striking summit forms (Kugy).   Kugy's pioneering in the Julian Alps excelled on Montasio and 8 or 9 independent rtes. or major variations are attributed to him.   Montasio is the second highest summit in the Julian Alps and on the whole is superior in form and interest to Triglav, although difficult to compare because of the former's unique N face.   The mtn. appears relatively simple on viewing its S face aspect from the huge sloping plain of the Altipiano del Montasio.   From here the normal and much the shortest rte. is taken and probably accounts for 9 out of 10 ascents today.   The W face or Dogna rte. offers the most remote and savage approach, up the Montasio-Clapadorie gorge, involving a big vertical interval and bivouacking in the classic tradition.   The spectacular NNW ridge, called Cresta dei Draghi (Dragons), divides the Clapadorie side from the impressive N/NE face above Saisera/Valbruna.   With an average height of 800m., it is half as high again as the S face, much longer, and divided in the summit line by two flying buttresses.   This N side offers two 'ordinary' rtes, apart from an original Kugy rte. which turns the Dragons ridge to reach the upper part of the W face.   All these rtes. are serious and noted for rte. finding problems.   The Suringar biv. hut (2430m.) is situated on the great ledge topping the main part of the W face;   a cave called the Muschi biv. is found at the base of the W wall.   The Stuparich biv. hut (1587m.) is a useful forward base for climbing the N face, while there is a tiny emergency shelter below the summit on the ESE ridge.
   First ascent: H. Findenegg with A. Brussofier, 18 August, 1877.   In winter: J. Kugy with A. Oitzinger and G. Pesamosca, 6 February, 1905.

South Side and East-South-East Ridge (Via Brazzà).   The normal and easiest rte., resulting from an engineered and partly equipped path, so making it simpler than the original rte.   Paths across the lower part of the Montasio plain on all maps are somewhat incorrect in disposition, but the single upper track in its last km. to foot of S face is accurate. Steep in places with some exposure, hard snow slopes possible. Gr. I.

130. From the Brazzà hut follow a path N (another goes NE) for 3 min. to another path going in the same direction. Cross this L (NW) and follow a discontinuous track in a slightly rising traverse NW for nearly one km. over grass and a few stones running down in lateral ribs over the Montasio plain until the fairly obvious dry bed of the central plain stream is reached. Cross this to reach a path on the other side. (This path comes up from the lane end above the Pecol chalets at pt. 1576m., where its start is vague, but the stream bed can be followed for a min. or two until it is located). Now follow the path due N up the Montasio plain on the L side of the bed, along a grassy rib then up steeper slopes trending L with a few zigzags to contour just below the saddle of the Forca dei Disteis (2201m.). By a traverse movement R on scree go down a little to a way-marked fork under steep snowbeds lapping below the S face (2 h.).

Take the R branch over rubble and grass to slant R from just above a little rock projection along a broken terrace system, steep at first then in easier rising stretches over a path in places hewn from the rock to reach terraces under a large scree/snow field at the R side of the S face, below the Forca Verde. This screefield is reached from its R-hand end and is ascended easily to below an obvious L-hand gully rising from its head. Ignore this and slant R up steep grassy rocks, track discontinuous, and so turn triangular rock mass and tower to R of gully. So reach the col above (2587m.) (1 h.). Turn the tower above on its R side along ledges, pass across the head of the gully and keep to L side of the crest, faded way-marks, where care should be taken. Reach a large waymark indicating an exit from below. (This comes up from the 'ladder' variation, which takes the outer L wall of the gully below the col; 60m. of metal ladder then cables to reach the usual rte.

JÖF DI MONTASIO S side

Modeon del Montasio 2606
2573
F. Berdo 2530
Cima Verde 2661
Forca Verde 2587
scree/snow field
ladder
2680
130
Upper ledges
130
130
2753
crux
132
Lower ledges
Torre Disteis 2468
131
Findenegg ledge
Forca dei Disteis
2201
2241
1961
Altipiano del Montasio
130

on ridge; a short cut, very exposed and not for the squeamish; avoid in doubtful weather or when other parties are above).

Continue up a steeper ridge section with a rock hewn track and metal spikes to pt. 2680m. Now follow the straightforward crest to a slight depression where a broader ridge rises to the summit (45 min., $3\frac{3}{4}$ h. from Brazzà hut).

Original (Findenegg) Route. This traverses L over the lower ledges of the S face on to the W face and exits up a large gully. Altogether more serious than Via Brazzà with steep snow ribbons and some loose rock. Old waymarks and cairns, and remains of old cables and spikes. Gr. II.

131. Follow Rte. 130 to the waymarked fork under the S face (2 h.). Take the L branch with a few steep zigzags up the fading rib above the saddle towards the wall where a narrow inlet is closed by a water-stained alcove. Move L below this across a snowband, delicate, to reach the entrance to the lower ledges rising L across the face. Follow a little track over progressive terraces to a fine position under the Disteis tower, where the face turns SW. Horizontally in the same line continue by very narrow ledges (Findenegg Ledge) interrupted by hard snow tongues, delicate, some fixed aids in place. In 180m. distance go round a corner on to the W face and still barely rising continue for nearly the same distance to a large red painted arrow waymark on a broader ledge (1 h.). (About 50m. further along the next series of broken terraces, slightly higher and at the apex of the W face terraces, the Suringar biv. hut will be found). Above the arrow climb up narrowing rock shelves direct into a big obvious gully cutting the face above. There are narrower gullies on either side. In the lower bed of the Findenegg Gully hard snow may be found, up to a fork; keep to R side, old waymarks on retaining wall. Climb the bed of the L branch on loose rock with two steep pitches and exit on the NNW ridge about 5 min. from summit

(45 min., $3\frac{3}{4}$ h. from Brazzà hut).

132. <u>South-West Pillar (Direct Kugy Route)</u>. The classic rte. on S side of mtn., notable for its short crux pitch, somewhat excessive for the climb as a whole. Fairly good rock with a few loose sections. There are several variations on the upper pillar section, at least one of which is easier than the original line. See rte. diagram. Mainly IV with one pitch of V- high up. G. Bolaffio and J. Kugy with A. Oitzinger and O. Pesamosca, 29 August, 1908.

133. <u>North Face Italian Hunters' Route (Via Amalia)</u>. Waymarked and equipped in the 1950s. Very steep, above a snow/ice slope, some stonefall danger, 600m. to N shoulder (2458m.) from where a ledge traverse is taken across the upper W face past the Suringar biv. hut to join Rte. 131. Gr. II ($4\frac{1}{2}$ h. from foot of face to summit, plus $2\frac{1}{2}$ h. from Grego hut, or 45 min. from Stuparich biv. hut).

134. <u>North Face Kugy Direct Route</u>. Probably the most continuously equipped rte. in the Julian Alps; nevertheless an outstanding expedition, relatively short in duration because of extensive aid on many pitches. It starts up the R side of the flying buttress descending L of the summit line, and higher up follows closely along the buttress crest. Glacier recession and an icy crevasse under the face where the climb starts is making access to the first pitch more difficult. 700m., Gr. II+ ($3\frac{1}{2}$ h. from foot of face, plus 3 h. from Grego hut, or $1\frac{1}{4}$ h. from Stuparich biv. hut).

JÔF FUART   2666m.

135.   Slov: Višnja gora.   Ger: Wischberg = strong or high mtn.   The main summit of the easterly section of the W Julians.

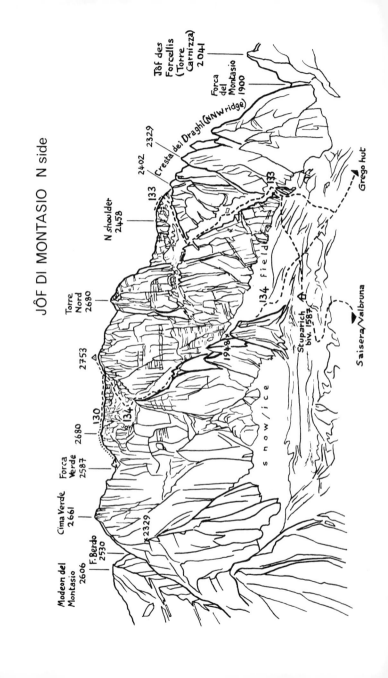

JÖF DI MONTASIO N side

Modeon del Montasio 2606
F. Berdo 2550
Cima Verde 2661
Forca Verde 2587
2680
130
134
× 2329
2753
Torre Nord 2680
1948
N shoulder 2458
133
2402
Cresta dei Draghi (NNW ridge) 2329
133
Jöf des Forcellis (Torre Carnizza) 2041
Forca del Montasio 1900
134 field
Stuparich biv. 1587
snow/ice
Grego hut
Saisera/Valbruna

It commands an array of limestone spires and towers without equal for interest in the Julian Alps, almost exclusively visited and known to Ital. climbers. There are normal rtes. of Gr. I/II on the S (Corsi hut, $2\frac{3}{4}$ h.) and N (Pellarini hut, 4 h.) sides of the main summit, and several outstanding pillar and wall climbs averaging 600-800m. Among the numerous satellite towers, with normal rtes. on good rock seldom below Gr. II/III, and classic rtes. of IV/V+, are: Campanile di Villaco (Villacherturm), 2247m.; Cima de lis Codis (Spranjeturm), 2380m.; Torre delle Madri dei Camosci (Gamsmutterturm), 2503m.; Cima di Riofreddo (Kaltwassergamsmutter), 2507m. Further E and closer to Cave del Predil village, less elevated but equally notable for fine rock climbing, rises the Riobianco group, including: Cima del Vallone (Korspitze), 2368m.; Cime Grande (and Piccola) della Scala (Grosse Leiterspitze), 2242m.; Vetta Bella (Schönkopf), 2049m.; Cima delle Cenge (Hochstelle), 2007m.; Cima Alta di Riobianco (Hohe Weissenbachspitze), 2257m. Due to the favourable siting of biv. type huts the approaches to most of these peaks are short. First known ascent of Jôf Fuart, about 1850.

Note: The PZS map is very inaccurate in this zone, while the IGM map is not altogether good and suffers from omission of detail.

Triglav from Razor

Supplement 1990

Political and economic upheaval in Yugoslavia has led to civil unrest, riots and 3-figure inflation in the 1980s (900% in 1989). The Dinar/Sterling exchange rate in 1977 was 30; in 1989, 100,000. In a complex ethnic melting pot of nationalism rising among the various federated states that constitute modern Yugoslavia, Slovenia alone has a degree of economic strength and is threatening to secede from the union as a whole. It is no secret that as an independent state and following a plebiscite the public vote would go in favour of uniting with Austria - by whom they were once occupied and with whom they share the commonly understood German language. The processes of shedding traditional communism in neighbouring Hungary also raises the spectre of a mini-power block and association of countries resembling in boundaries the former Austo-Hungarian Empire. This would become an obvious target for EEC membership.

These political changes would have a profound effect on the mobility of visitors; but possibly not before bloody revolution intervened in the case of Slovenia and its growing estranged relationship with the rest of the country.

Unique for a European country in modern times, a number of "Third-world malpractices" in tourism have come into use. Chief among these are shopping and many services (eg meals) in centres set aside for visitors where only "hard currencies" are taken; costs and charges can be 5 times higher than equivalents for residents. Visitors are advised that some of the well known ways round these "rip-offs" may contravene currency and other legislation regulations. In Slovenia, and especially the Julian Alps, great efforts have been made to ignore official procedures ordered from Belgrade, and foreigners are treated as far as possible like residents. The military has threatened the Slovenes in some of these matters, and numerous "incidents" have been reported.

Not surprisingly, the modern package tour offered by the large travel operators in Britain and other European countries has been widely adopted by holidaymakers as the most economic and practical way of visiting the Julian Alps in the 1980s. Tourist centres for the main holiday companies are now well established in Kranjska Gora, Bled and Bovec. Bled in particular is now invaded by hordes of trippers, though attempts to get Kranjska Gora going as an international winter sports centre have so far stagnated. Mountain walkers can buy a package tour for periods ranging from a week, to 10 days or for 2 or 3 weeks, and on reaching the destination go their own way. However, it is wasteful if travelling say on a half-board package arrangement when you possibly plan to be away from your hotel in the mountains for at least half the time, using huts for accommodation which have to be paid for additionally. Therefore consider booking only bed and breakfast or self catering packages, depending on precise plans. Public transport is still good and cheap in Slovenia, for getting round from valley to valley, etc. Car hire is very expensive.

Camping addicts will have to make their own way - possibly at greater expense if travelling by air as it is difficult to find spare (cheap) charter seats as a rule to Ljubljana which contravenes local regulations about flying without some pre-booked accommodation paid for. The most economical approach for motorists remains via Venice Marco Polo airport or the military standby one and carhire from there - though now quite expensive even on fly-drive schemes.

Authorised campsites with good though variable facilities exist at Bovec, Bled lake W end (Zaka), Bohinj lake S side and W end, Gozd Martuljek, Trenta. In Italy, Tarvisio and at N end of the Predil lake. As previously, a number of unauthorised sites can be found especially in important access valleys.

Guidebooks

See p.26. The old PZS **Triglav** booklet was reissued as a little pocket book in 1979, **How to climb Triglav.** It contains descriptions of walking (not climbing) routes on Triglav alone, with notes on access, flora, fauna etc. and numerous colour pictures.
Triglav National Park. Bled, 1987. A comprehensive cultural guide to the national park.

Huts and other facilities

See pp.43-62. With a UIAA reciprocal rights card cut-price accommodation rates in huts was still only £2.50 in 1989 for basic dormitory sleeping; bunks and rooms will cost more. Several huts have been enlarged, with improved facilities and greater sleeping capacity, eg. the Prehodavcih (p.55) now has 50 places and a full restaurant service.

pp.30,60. Prestreljenik cableway at Bovec. In the 1980s this chairlift has in general only operated at weekends.

Maps

See pp.24-25. Severe material shortages of the 1980s have taken their toll on the reliable availability of Slovene topographic mapping, while in Italy government military mapping (IGM) has been withdrawn from public sale altogether. The latter should not now be sought, although an open invitation exists for a commercial publisher to apply for a licence to copy official mapping. Meanwhile the PZS 50M sheet Julian West must suffice for the West Julian Italian zone summits. Those who failed to secure mapping before leaving for the area have sometimes found the local tourist offices in Bovec, Kranjska Gora and Bled closed during the summer in recent years owing to strikes. In the past these offices have been a source for some maps.

Following publication of the PZS 20M Bohinj map, a complementary 20M sheet in the same format, entitled Triglav, was issued in 1984 (current edition 1988); this adjoins the N side of the Bohinj sheet, and the 2 together cover about one quarter of the area represented in the PZS 50M Julian East map.

Using the same style as PZS 50M, an additional PZS 50M map entitled Triglavski Narodni Park was published in 1983 (current edition 1987); it extends further W than PZS Julian East, to include Bovec, but loses a comparable amount of ground at the E (Bled) edge while barely touching Kranjska Gora in the N. The reverse side of this map is covered with very basic tourist information of no particular value in several languages including English.

Another map of 50M by GZ Ljubljana, based on the military topographic survey (better and worse in variable respects than PZS), was put out in 1986, first as Bohinj, Bled and Surrounding (sic), then revised in 1988 as Gorenjska - Bled - Bohinj - Kranjska Gora. It covers an area similar to the PZS 50M park map but is aligned 10km further E so that, for instance, Bovec in the W is a long way off the sheet. The reverse side of this map has superior tourist information in English and other languages.

Round Bovec, and occasionally found for sale in the Bovec tourist office, a specially cut out section of 25M from the military map with tourist information overprinted is a cherished possession of those who have managed to get a copy. It is particularly good for the Canin-Prestreljenik frontier ridge walks and routes.

The best road map now widely available is the RV 300M sheet entitled Yugoslav Coast. This is greatly oversized but cheap, well got up and handy for identifying all other important mountain areas in Yugoslavia.

When available all mapping is obtainable in the UK from West Col Productions.

Kugy monument in upper Trenta valley

Razor from Preval

Index